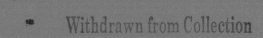

Temptress

*From
the Original
Bad Girls to
Women
on Top*

Temptress

Jane Billinghurst

GREYSTONE BOOKS
Douglas & McIntyre Publishing Group
VANCOUVER / TORONTO / BERKELEY / NEW YORK

To Tom for his delight and the Wildcats for theirs

Greystone Books
A division of Douglas & McIntyre Ltd.
2323 Quebec Street, Suite 201
Vancouver, British Columbia
Canada V5T 4S7
www.greystonebooks.com

NATIONAL LIBRARY OF CANADA CATALOGUING IN PUBLICATION DATA

Billinghurst, Jane, 1958-
   Temptress : from the original bad girls to women on top / Jane Billinghurst.

   Includes bibliographical references and index.
   ISBN 1-55054-999-5

   1. Femmes fatales. 2. Women in popular culture—History. I. Title.
HQ1122.B58 2003   305.42'09   C2003-910364-1

Library of Congress information is available upon request

Editing by Nancy Flight
Copy editing by Pamela Robertson
Jacket illustration *Lilith* by John Collier. Courtesy Atkinson Art Gallery, Southport, Lancashire, U.K.
Jacket and interior design by Peter Cocking and Val Speidel
Printed and bound in China by C.S. Graphics Pte. Ltd.
Printed on acid-free paper
Distributed in the U.S. by Publishers Group West

We gratefully acknowledge the financial support of the Canada Council for the Arts, the British Columbia Arts Council, and the Government of Canada through the Book Publishing Industry Development Program (BPIDP) for our publishing activities.

Every effort has been made to trace accurate ownership of copyright text and visual material used in this book. Errors or omissions will be corrected in subsequent editions, provided notification is sent to the publisher.

Contents

Introduction: Sizzle 1

1   The Original Bad Girls *15*

2   Mythical Maidens *27*

3   Cleopatra *41*

4   Mistresses *57*

5   Subversive Seductresses *75*

6   The Vamp *93*

7   The Bombshell *105*

8   The Femme Fatale *115*

9   The Sex Kitten *127*

10   The Matron and the Nymphet *135*

11   The Ultimate Bitch *147*

12   Women on Top *157*

Notes *173*
Bibliography *177*
Illustration Credits *180*
Index *181*

facing page: In the 1981 movie *Body Heat,* Kathleen Turner's character leads her victim astray, then leaves him to his fate while she savors her freedom on a sun-drenched beach.

Introduction

Sizzle

A tall, cool blonde in a white dress threads her way through a darkly sweating crowd. From the oppressive shadows at the edge of the evening, a man watches, then follows her to the railing along a boardwalk. Standing slightly apart, the couple leans toward the night ocean. Even here, at the edge of the water, there is no relief from the heat. He offers to buy her a drink, and she says she'll take a cone of shaved ice. Cherry.

As the conversation nudges forward, he remarks that she looks well tended and says that he wouldn't mind being tended himself. She recommends marriage. When he replies that he meant being tended just for the night, she laughs and chokes on her ice cone. Red-tinted crystals fall from the paper cup and a crimson stain spreads across the front of her dress. As he sets off to get her a paper towel, she turns to face him. "You don't want to lick it?" she challenges. In that instant, every nerve in his body goes into overdrive. By the time he returns, she is gone from the boardwalk but firmly etched in his mind.

It is 1981, and the movie is *Body Heat,* starring William Hurt as Ned Racine and Kathleen Turner as Matty Walker. In the opening scenes of the movie, we watch as Ned becomes a stepping stone in Matty's personal journey to an earthly paradise. She will lead him to believe that he is the driving force behind their plan to murder her husband and make away with his millions. Only when Ned is sitting in his prison cell at the end of the movie does he realize that Matty sought him out as the man most likely to get her what she wants.

Why does Ned go along with her criminal plan? The answer is simple: he has fallen victim to a temptress, a woman who emanates such a strong field of attraction that it disrupts a man's view of the world. Instead of using his intellect to examine his experiences, he responds viscerally to the primal forces he senses in that oh-so-cool blonde (or brunette or black-haired) beauty. The underlying message is that intellectual responses to experience are what hold the world together; once Ned sets the filter of reason aside, there is nowhere to go but down.

Matty leaps off the screen the moment we see her and sears herself into Ned's consciousness. To get Ned thinking he might be able to take advantage of her charms, she delivers the line about licking the red ice crystals off the front of her dress. Skilled temptresses know that, consciously or unconsciously, the radar of the male mind is always scanning for signs that a woman might be available to him. The more desirable the woman, the more it will mean to him to score. If she will have him, he must be special indeed.

Matty lets Ned know that she has singled him out above all the others. When he tracks her down at her local bar—as she knew he would—she tells him that the other men in the room would kill to sit on the bar stool next to her, but she would never let them. When Matty and Ned make love, she makes it clear how much she wants him and that only he is man enough to fully satisfy the hugely desirable creature that she is. Finally, she gives him to understand that she desperately needs his help. She is only a woman. What can she do? If she is going to survive in this world, she needs a big strong protector by her side. What man could resist such deliciously satisfying strokes to his ego and his body? He doesn't stop to ask himself what Matty might be getting out of the arrangement—presumably the joy of being with him is sufficient to satisfy her desires.

The moment Ned accepts Matty's version of reality, he steps off the precipice. He has ignored the warning signs. And there have been a few: Matty's appetite for sex is perhaps a little too voracious; other men whose levels of testosterone are not quite so elevated in her presence can almost taste danger, and have told him so. Once Matty has led Ned to the brink, however, his powers of reasoning are no match for his visceral responses to her allure. He brushes off his friends' warnings and makes that fatal move. "You're not too smart, are you?" Matty observes at one point. "I like that in a man."

When Ned steps into the void, his descent takes an agonizingly long time. Piece by intricate piece, Matty's master plan is revealed, but the full horror of her machinations becomes clear only after she has gone too far to be stopped—and even then the depths of her depravity are known only to her victim. Ned's pain at the end of the movie is all the greater because he is the only one who understands how successful she has been.

In the final shot of *Body Heat,* Matty relaxes on a tropical beach as an attractive young male waiter serves her a long, cool drink. She is clearly biding her time, waiting in delicious languor until she feels the urge to upset another man's world—for there are always men who will fall for a woman like Matty.

MEN, THE DESIGNATED storytellers for most of history, are the keepers of temptress tales. Depending on the era in which these tales are told, temptresses may be vicious and deadly, or they may be attractive diversions from, but no real threat to, men's main task of ruling the world. Just how temptresses are presented all depends on how confident the storytellers are about male supremacy. When men feel strong, temptresses are lusty and full of life. When men feel weak, temptresses are chilling predators with chaos on their minds.

Throughout history, the balance of power between the sexes has fluctuated, but for as long as we have had records it has always favored men. Ambitious women have had to create their own success. Some retreat to cloistered female worlds where women advance by default. Others challenge men directly, sometimes even joining their ranks. In the 1700s, Anne Bonney plied her trade as a pirate. One hundred years later, when women were barred from becoming doctors in England, Miranda Stuart became James Barry and rose to become inspector-general of military hospitals. Her deception was discovered when she died, and the military funeral planned in her honor was abruptly canceled.

Then there are those women who, observing how men's eyes instinctively slide down over the curve of a breast or up over the smooth slope of a calf, hang their fortunes on the very feature that sets them apart from men: their femininity. Historically, temptresses have weighed their disadvantaged position in patriarchal society against their natural attributes and have

4

decided that if they play their cards right, they can come out ahead. The temptress can do this because men respond so beautifully just to the idea of sex. All the woman needs to do is create the expectation of delight, and the man will willingly part with money and power. In the tales men tell, a skilled temptress can even get away with murder.

The way men envision the temptress dictates how women can use the role to their advantage. When men are confident of their supremacy, witty, accomplished women can use powerful men to improve their social standing. The men indulge their delightful temptresses, safe in the knowledge that their power base will remain intact. In Renaissance Italy and Restoration England, for example, courtesans could tempt men in the upper echelons of society to part with some of their fortunes in return for amusing conversation and diverting sex. The men could boast to their fellow men of the beauties they had snagged, while the women could live in luxury and create their own spheres of influence among the social elite. There was just enough intrigue to spice the relationship but not enough to spoil the fun.

When men are less sure of their continued position of superiority but women are not poised to rock the boat, temptresses remain delightful, but men are less interested in women's wit and accomplishments (which could be viewed as threatening) and concentrate instead on women's physical attributes (which never cease to entertain). If the age requires it, there are always women willing to downplay their brainpower and focus on simple, unadulterated sex. As Mae West once commented, "Brains are an asset to the woman . . . who's smart enough to hide 'em."

Women admired for their bodies rather than their wit often affect child-like dispositions to suggest just how easy they would be to dominate. To be sure, many of them still have their eyes on the man's wallet, but in return he gets fun-filled nights free of philosophical discussion. If he does have to part with money or make some kind of commitment, it is worth it. He gets physical gratification and the chance to show off his prize to his friends.

The childlike seductress exists mainly as a visual delight. She is perfect as a fantasy figure because she comes with so few strings attached. And from the woman's point of view, this method of seduction really isn't all that much work. As long as her face and figure conform to prevailing standards of beauty, all she has to do is undulate gently and reveal slightly more flesh than is decent, and the males in the audience she is playing to are hooked.

The sex kitten is the least threatening of all temptress types: willing to be subordinate once she has her man and easy to leave once the first flush of desire has subsided. These women—as you may already have guessed— are often blonde. They were especially celebrated by filmmakers in the fifties, when men realized—to their immense relief—that the male-dominated social hierarchy had survived the upheavals of World War II and women had not seized the moment to start running things back home (or, at least, not anything that mattered).

Both the confident courtesan and the sex kitten are temptresses for eras when the male-dominated social hierarchy is working well. There are times, however, when the system is not running smoothly—or at least when men fear it might go off the rails. These may be times when women are seeking to improve their status or periods of general societal unrest. When storm clouds gather, the temptress's sunny delights are quickly replaced by darker intentions.

There has always been the pervasive feeling that men, the rational sex, impose order, whereas women, the emotional sex, subvert it. Men control

nature, whereas women collude with it. When there is a general nervousness about where the civilized world is headed, storytellers remind men of women's connection with the world's naturally chaotic state. They tell tales of what happens when women tempt men from the straight and narrow.

The femme fatale of the 1940s film noir is this kind of temptress. She finds a victim and uses him to pursue a selfish plan. Such tales serve as an advance warning system: there's potential danger, but if men stick together, the situation should not get out of control. To underscore this point, the storytellers make sure that the wayward dame—along with the poor man she has duped—gets her comeuppance in the end.

If women as a group do not press their demands aggressively, men are content to tell stories of temptresses who fail. Sometimes, however, unsettling world events coincide with militant action or actual progress from the ranks of women and blood pressures rise. Fearful about the chaos that might ensue were women to gain power at men's expense and against men's will, men translate the image of women agitating for rights and recognition (or achievement of the same) into the image of women whose sexual lust is insatiable.

Unlike the femme fatale, who has her eyes set on a personal victory within the male-dominated system, the temptress in times of male paranoia is portrayed as a black hole, sucking in all the maleness around her. These women will bleed men dry and reduce them to mere husks of their former selves. Once the men are sufficiently weakened, the women will swoop in and take over, brushing the masculine shadows aside. Men's hair stands on end when they think of what such insurrection might mean, and images of beautiful but deadly female vampires and psychopaths leak out of their collective thoughts.

As women made social and political gains, sexual interplay—and temptress storytelling—became more equal. In the twentieth century, women such as the irrepressible Mae West and the ever-inventive Madonna began to strut their own suggestions for temptress fantasies across the collective male consciousness. Those men who realized that social and political gains made by women were not necessarily achieved at their expense relaxed and discovered what extra delights could be offered by women who accepted the hard wiring of their men as a potential source of pleasure rather than as the seat of male dominance. Feminine beauty and intelligence no longer coalesced into the image of the psychopath or femme fatale but became part of a package of adventurous sexuality just waiting to be explored with the satisfaction of both partners in mind. No matter who the storyteller is, however, to retain her edge, the temptress has to contain at least some element of risk, some sense of the forbidden, some sense of danger.

ALL TEMPTRESS STORIES are echoes of the original stories men told to justify their superior position in society. The mirror of history reflects a male-dominated world, but it was not always so. Tantalizing fragments from before the Bronze Age suggest a time when partnership between the sexes may have been the norm, when women were revered for the important and very visible part they played in continuing the human race. There are many theories about what happened to change this state of affairs, but it is clear that once men became the recognized authorities, they created stories to explain why it was only right and fitting that they, rather than women, should be the ones in charge. These stories were handed down over

generations and eventually became incorporated into early records, such as the Old Testament and Greek mythology.

These earliest temptress tales tell of a time before the arrival of woman when all was right with the world. Hardship, the male storytellers suggest, is the woman's fault. In such stories, sex is key. If the woman hadn't batted her eyelashes, exposed that delicately turned ankle, pushed forward those softly mounded breasts, men could be in paradise still. But no, women used sex to get men to lose control. The temptress stories remind men of this. Oh, there are times when losing oneself completely in that moment of orgasm can seem worth any price, but, the storytellers implore, think of the consequences! One transitory moment of delight can lead to a lifetime of trouble, and women are just waiting for the opportunity to make this happen.

facing page: Beneath a cool, calm exterior there lurks in every woman—or so a man hopes—a red-hot lover just waiting to be released. In temptresses, passion flows so close to the surface that passing men can feel the heat. ROWENA, *ON THE SURFACE*, 1990s.

The temptress is a composite of fact and fancy created by men and exploited by women. When men are comfortable with the status quo (either because they are not threatened by strong women or because women are so subservient that the social hierarchy is unlikely to change), they conjure up images of delicious women intent on satisfying their every whim. As men's confidence levels decline, temptresses become increasingly dangerous. When women seem poised to upset the balance of power between the sexes, men fear that temptresses will turn on them. In times like these, men conjure up images of deadly temptresses intent on chaos and destruction.

Yet no matter where the temptresses fall on the spectrum from delicious to deadly, they retain their appeal. Delightful temptresses are worth the detour because the dalliance is pleasant and does not entail much risk. Deadly temptresses are worth an abrupt change of course because as the level of risk rises, so does the anticipated level of satisfaction. That is why spending one night in Cleopatra's bed, even though it meant losing one's life in the morning, is a fantasy that delights rather than appalls. When one has experienced the ultimate in bliss, what point is there in continuing to live?

This book documents the ever-changing shape of seductive beauty. It shows how women historically have used male temptress fantasies to their own advantage and how women in modern times have increasingly taken a hand in defining the fantasy itself. The ideal of the temptress can wake men up with wet dreams or cold sweats; the temptress can be an image projected by men onto women or an adventure of shared desire. This book traces her electric image as charged particles of desire and sexual politics form and reform in misty curtains of light that dance across the night-sky darkness of world events.

Chapter 1

The Original Bad Girls

Lilith

In an image painted by the British artist John Collier in 1887, the red-blonde hair of a naked young woman cascades to her waist as she caresses a serpent that is slowly and deliberately entwining itself around her silken thighs. The snake has made its way up the curve of her back and dropped its muscular body down over her shoulder, stopping to flicker its tongue above her breasts. The woman's ankles are bound by a twist of the creature's tail, and she presses her cheek against the diamond wedge of its head, complicit in its exploration of her person. The dreamy Lilith is obviously familiar with this lustrous creature, on such intimate terms with it that her caress is almost absentminded. Feeling its weight upon her body, she rides the wave of pleasure that the touch of scale on skin creates. The huge size of the muscular snake holds no threat, and the soft ripple of serpentine flesh molds itself perfectly to her body. Lilith and the phallic symbol of evil are held in a perfect balance by the artist's brush.

Male painters of Victorian England were fascinated by the independent sexuality of Eve's predecessor and Adam's first wife, the mysterious Lilith. Created Adam's equal, according to medieval Jewish folkore, Lilith was appalled when her husband insisted on the missionary position for sex. She knew she had been made from the same clay that he had, and she wanted an equal say in how their love life unfolded. She wanted to experiment with this new flesh, to explore the range of pleasures it could provide.

Adam, in contrast, was rather a prude. The idea of creating a sexual dialogue, of reacting to the signs fed back to his body from Lilith's, of following an impulse not knowing where it might lead, was foreign to him. He did not yet know enough about his own urges to feel comfortable abandoning himself to Lilith's. He refused to listen to his wife, and Lilith submitted to night after night of missionary sex—her mind, no doubt, on other things, like the wide expanse of the night sky, the rustling of creatures in the bushes . . . and the possibilities of life without Adam.

Resentment built in Lilith until she could stand it no longer. Undaunted by the fact that she knew nothing about the world outside paradise, according to the text of *The Alphabet of Ben Sira,* she "uttered the ineffable name of God," the gates of Eden swung open, and off she went to make her own way in the world, unencumbered by her sexually unimaginative husband.

Lilith's life from then on has been portrayed as one long party. She went to the Red Sea, where she cavorted with all manner of hideous demons, indulging in whatever sexual positions she wanted and producing hundreds of demon children. When Adam complained to God that his supposed helpmeet had left him, God sent three angels to bring Lilith back to where she belonged. But she refused to return: she had found a place where she could indulge her sexuality, and she had no regrets.

Despite her new lifestyle, Lilith never completely severed her ties with the uptight male to whom she had once been married. After Adam lost his immortality and begat humankind, Lilith started taking the lives of young children, creeping in at night through open windows and snatching their breath away. When unsuspecting parents tried to wake their offspring, they found that their previously healthy babies had died in the night. The three angels were horrified by such heartless, vindictive behavior. They could not force Lilith to return to Eden, but they did strike a bargain with her. Her window of opportunity for such malicious behavior was restricted to eight days after birth for baby boys and twenty days for baby girls. In addition, if amulets were hung inscribed with the angels' names—Senoy, Sansenoy, and Semangelof—Lilith agreed to stay away.

Strangling babies while they slept was not Lilith's only revenge against the man who had denied her pleasure. She also wafted into the dreams of men who slept alone. A slight rub of skin on skin or skin on sheet, and the men could not help but react physically to the thoughts she conjured up. The wet dream was her gift to the sons of Adam. A slight morning stickiness, proof of the nocturnal emission, was often the only sign of her visit—and a yearning to remember just what pleasure it was that she had promised as she passed by.

Lilith lingers in the thoughts of men as a reminder of sexual opportunities lost or not yet found. Here was a woman who was not afraid to take charge, who could imagine delights of which Adam could not conceive. To abandon oneself to the charms of such a woman—who knows where that might lead? Men have been wondering ever since.

Phyllis and Aristotle

. . . .

A FAVORITE cautionary tale in the thirteenth century on the importance of men keeping their passions in check was the story of Aristotle and the object of his desire—the whip-wielding Phyllis. In this tale, as told by the thirteenth-century Norman poet Henri d'Andeli, Aristotle was in the employ of Alexander the Great. The elderly philosopher had told the young king to curb his passion for his mistress, Phyllis, in case frivolous lovemaking distracted him from the serious task of military conquest.

The luscious Phyllis was none too pleased at having her pleasure rationed, and she plotted her revenge. Aristotle began to encounter Phyllis in the palace corridors in various states of undress and dishevelment. And there she was again, idling in the palace gardens outside his study window. Among the heady scents of flowers in a riot of colors, she sang softly as she wandered about in her gossamer chemise.

The tantalizing glimpses of fair flesh worked their magic on the aged Aristotle, and he begged Phyllis to sate his desire. She said she would if he would first agree to come crawling into the garden on hands and knees so that she could saddle him up and ride him around like a horse. By now, Aristotle was in no state to refuse her anything, and into the garden he crawled. Phyllis mounted him and gave a triumphant whoop, causing Alexander to look out of his window.

Alexander was incensed at what he saw. He accused his teacher of warning him away from Phyllis because he wanted her for himself. Aristotle may have been no match for Phyllis, but he did have wit enough to reason his way out of his tight spot with Alexander. He told the king that if he—an old man—had been duped by Phyllis, how much more important was it that Alexander—a young one—keep his hands off her and on the reins of power?

Eve

As part of his work on the Sistine Chapel ceiling for Pope Julius II, Michelangelo painted *The Fall of Man and the Expulsion from the Garden of Eden* in 1509 and 1510. In this scene, a female serpent is coiled around the Tree of Knowledge, which separates two images: one showing Adam and Eve in the Garden of Eden, the other showing them being banished from paradise. In the garden, Adam reaches out his hand to pluck an apple from the tree, his legs braced apart to steady his stance, while Eve sits on the ground before him, her face between his thighs. The image suggests that before the Fall, along with the world of knowledge promised by the apple, Lilith's successor opened up for Adam a whole new world of physical sensation.

When plotting the fall of humankind, the wily serpent avoided Adam, knowing that this upright, rational man would refuse to compromise his idyllic situation and his position with God. But Eve was different. She was more open to suggestion, more curious, less interested in the rules. Most important, she connected with Adam on a level that bypassed his rational wiring and plugged directly into his intense, reflexive responses to the sight and sound of her.

Adam could catch his wife's distinctive scent even in the heavy, flower-laden air of Eden. When she stepped up quietly behind him and held him close, the hairs on the back of his neck rose to meet the moist warmth of her breath. When he saw her bending to pick flowers or rounding a corner down a forest path, the soft curve of her hips beckoned. This was something the serpent could work with. He told Eve about the apple, but he also initiated her into the delights of sex and suggested how she could use her newfound knowledge on her husband.

Eve beckoned and Adam came. Since the day that Adam succumbed to his wife's persuasive charm, the name Eve has been synonymous with sexual temptation. "You are [each] an Eve," thundered the theologian Tertullian in the second century as he exhorted women to keep their sexual natures in check. The moment they spread their legs, men were lost. "You are the devil's gateway," he assured them. "You are she who persuaded him whom the devil was not valiant enough to attack." Certain early Christian groups echoed Tertullian's concerns: "The Prince of Darkness and his companions created Eve also after the like manner, imparting to her of their own lust, with a view to the deceiving of Adam."

Biblical passages confirm the scholars' view that men have long been bothered by women who promise them sexual delight. Proverbs 7 tells of gorgeous creatures who wait on street corners, stepping out of the shadows to seize men and shower them with kisses. They lure men back to soft beds decked out in bright colors and scented with aphrodisiacal perfumes. In dens of silken cushions, these women devoted themselves to giving men pleasure. In Isaiah 3:16–18 and 4, men are warned that the daughters of Zion walk "glancing wantonly with their eyes, mincing along as they go, tinkling with their feet." To save men, God will strip them of all adornments, the tools of their seductive trade. Even disarmed, however, women remain dangerous.

Early Christian men who had to greet women during church services by shaking their hands were advised to first wrap their hands in their robes to shield their flesh against their seductive touch.

Before the arrival of the Hebrews, the peoples of Canaan had worshipped goddesses who were quite unlike the virginal Madonna, the divinely inseminated mother of Christ who was venerated by the Roman Catholic Church in later ages. These Canaanite goddesses were fully realized sexual beings at a time when birth was interpreted as a divine mystery and people made offerings to the gods to appease the forces of nature. Once people believed a male God created the world through his word alone, the power of the feminine as an object of reverence declined, but the thread of sexuality linking the daughters of Eve to the ancient goddesses continued unbroken.

The power of women's sexuality unnerved biblical scribes and early church fathers alike. Women's sexuality engenders uncontrollable urges and unwanted erections, as the male body charts its own course in the sea of desire. In the moment of orgasm, the pilotless boat bucks and plunges as wave follows foam-topped wave. This is the moment of complete abandon that men both yearn for and fear. This is the moment when their bodies transport them on incredible journeys that their conscious minds cannot map. But they are also at the mercy of the ocean. They, the designated keepers of order, find themselves storm-tossed in chaos until the storm has blown itself out.

Eve, in their minds, is the keeper of this chaos, their portal into this world. Time and again, male artists place Eve in untended Edens, landscapes overrun with vigorous vegetation capable of smothering all traces of human progress. In the dark tropical jungles of the early twentieth-century French painter Henri Rousseau, or on the covers of such modern American fantasy

GREG HILDEBRANDT

magazines as *Heavy Metal*, Eve stands—or lies—naked, unafraid to look the serpent in the eye. The world of creeping tendrils and lush blooms, of rampant untamed nature, is the world where Eve belongs. She can still lead a man into this world of raw sensation—or so he fervently hopes.

THE STORIES handed down by early rabbis and fathers of the Christian church justified the suppression of women by reinforcing the idea that every woman carries within her the seeds of chaos. Holy men abstained from sex and did their utmost to banish all impure thoughts from their minds. Unfortunately, this was easier said than done. To keep passion in check, some starved themselves so that they had barely enough strength to live, let alone enough energy to fuel their libidos. Others fled into deserts far from the sights and sounds and smells of women, and whipped the flesh on their backs raw to keep physical sensations focused on pain rather than on pleasure.

In general, it was considered prudent to keep women out of sight—if not out of mind. One holy woman—Alexandra—had herself entombed alive so that she would not present a temptation to the young man who lusted after her. She whiled away the time waiting for death by praying and spinning flax. And one man—St. Simeon the Stylite—retreated to the top of a sixty-foot pillar, leaving strict instructions that women were not to come near the base in case their femininity contaminated the very air he breathed.

Despite these extreme measures, or perhaps because of them, sexual thoughts continued to infiltrate the minds of many holy men. St. Jerome writes in his autobiography that his holy meditations were often interrupted by ephemeral, beckoning prostitutes; St. Anthony, who lived in the fourth century and is considered the father of monasticism, sat in his cave in the Egyptian desert stoically enduring the seductive visions the Devil sent to tempt him.

Men have created elaborate rules and codes of conduct to regulate socially acceptable behavior when it comes to translating their thoughts into action, but the lava streams of passion bubble not far below the surface. Temptresses sense when the thin veneer of civilization is likely to be breached and are ready to take advantage of the eruption before contact with the atmosphere hardens the molten flow. Men, it seems, are hard-wired for sex—and temptresses count on them remaining true to their natures.

BORIS ©90

Chapter 2

Mythical Maidens

Whereas the tales told by early rabbis and Christian fathers warned men to avoid women to protect themselves from their depravity, many tales of the ancient Greeks described how a man might enjoy deliciously dangerous sex and emerge unscathed. The Greeks knew that they were treading on dangerous ground, for they had an Eve of their own, and her name was Pandora.

Pandora

In 1920, the Swiss expressionist painter Paul Klee sketched his vision of Pandora's box. On a table stands a vase, a traditional object for painters of still lifes. But in this sketch the vase is contained within vulval lips and at the base of its bowl lies a deep vaginal gash. There are some flowers in the vase, but from deep in the center—out of the vaginal cleft—evil-looking vapors rise and spew out into the room. To know Pandora, to open her box, is to unleash all manner of horrors. The man who enters this territory must tread with care lest he, like so many men before him—Eve's husband, Adam, and Pandora's husband, Epimetheus, to mention just two—find the world around him irrevocably altered for the worse.

It all started as a feud between the Titan Prometheus and the supreme god, Zeus. Prometheus had tricked Zeus into choosing a useless pile of bones rather than the meaty bits from a burnt animal offering. As punishment, Zeus decided to deprive men of fire. Prometheus, who had brought many good things to men—including knowledge of mathematics, writing, architecture, and metalworking, as well as how to use fire in the first place—decided that men should get their fire back. So he climbed up to the top of Mount Olympus and trapped a quantity of fire in a fennel stalk and took it back down to earth. Zeus was even angrier about this insolence than he had been about the burnt offering.

In revenge, Zeus asked the fire god, Hephaestus, to mix earth and water to make a beautiful young maiden. Then he asked his impish winged messenger, Hermes—a god often associated with chaos—to give her a shameless mind. When Pandora was ready, the goddesses of Olympus decked her out in finery, and Zeus sent this beauty to Prometheus's brother, the mortal Epimetheus, as a gift. Prometheus had warned Epimetheus never to accept a gift from Zeus in case it was a trick, but Epimetheus was so enchanted by the breathtaking vision before him that he promptly forgot Prometheus's advice.

Pandora, it turns out, was not the only gift that Epimetheus had incautiously accepted from the wily Zeus. He had also accepted delivery of a large earthenware storage jar (often incorrectly referred to by later storytellers as a box), which Zeus had warned him never to open. Epimetheus had been happy to set it aside, not suspecting for a moment that Zeus had given him the jar anticipating that Epimetheus would be unable to resist making the insatiably curious Pandora his wife. The all-too-mortal man just could not wait to get his hands on the divinely inspired beauty, and he welcomed into his house the agent of his destruction.

The Greek poet Hesiod gives us to understand that before the arrival of Pandora, men had lived happy, carefree lives on Earth. The story also goes that it was after Epimetheus had sex with Pandora that the famous jar-opening fiasco occurred. Had Epimetheus not been seduced by Pandora's beauty, he would have sent her right back to where she came from and the lid would have stayed firmly on the jar. But, alas, it was not to be.

Just as Adam had lived happily with God's injunction never to eat the fruit of the Tree of Knowledge, Epimetheus had never considered opening the jar. However, Pandora, like Eve, was consumed by curiosity. What good-ies could there be in this intriguing vessel? Whereas Eve took a bite out of the apple, Pandora took a peek inside the jar. The actions had similarly dire consequences. In the jar were all the evils in the world, which man had so far been spared from experiencing. Pandora saw the evils escaping and clapped the lid back on the jar just in time to retain the one thing that was left inside: Hope. (It's not clear what Hope was doing in a jar full of evils, but ancient gods do not need to explain their logic to mere mortals.) From that day on, because of the actions of the first woman, men were made to suffer.

For the ancient Greeks, however, this was not the end of the story. Surely there was some way that men could enjoy such tantalizing women as Pandora without losing everything. They began to spin tales of brave heroes who could outwit the temptresses they encountered. Many men would meet their doom under the seductive gaze of these lovely ladies, but the chosen few—the truly fearless and the truly great—would triumph, giving all men hope that one day they, too, might be able to fearlessly savor such delights.

The Sirens

As an illustration for a 1912 edition of *Aesop's Fables*, British artist Arthur Rackham drew the image of a huge female form rising up from the sea. She looks as though she is kneeling in the waves. Sheets of displaced ocean pour down over her outstretched arms and gleam off her triumphantly exposed breasts. She gazes down upon a small, bedraggled sailor who is standing all alone on the beach. Behind her we glimpse what remains of his boat. Were he to step into the water at this moment, the undertow caused by her sudden emergence would drag him down into the depths, where most of his companions already lie, awaiting the inevitable crush of sinking timbers as the ocean currents tear their boat apart.

For the ancient Greeks, many of the terrors of the deep were embodied in female form. In their Mediterranean lurked the deadly whirlpool Charybdis, who sucked boats down with relentless force, and the six-headed sea monster Scylla, who emerged from her cave to pluck sailors from passing ships and devour them. Then there were the Sirens, whose song was so achingly beautiful that men would do anything to find the source of such heavenly melodies, inevitably drowning in their quest for bliss. But in Greek myth one man, Odysseus, experiences the delights of the Sirens' song and survives.

Odysseus manages this feat thanks to the advice of the enchantress Circe—a temptress in her own right. Circe emanates such sexual magnetism that with a single glance she can suck every rational thought from passing men's minds. In 1893, British artist Arthur Hacker painted his view of Odysseus's sailors mesmerized by Circe as she sits before them and raises her arms above her head to expose her beautiful breasts. The men crawl toward her, crowding around to get a better look, completely oblivious to their

gradual physical transformation into grunting, hairy pigs.

Circe herself is unfazed by the men's transformation. A bronze statuette by twentieth-century sculptor Edgar Bertram Mackennal shows the enchantress coolly casting her spell while men lie at the base of her pedestal in paroxysms of desire. The nineteenth-century Belgian painter Félicien Rops took the image even further, painting a black-stockinged dominatrix taking a pig for a walk: man mastered, his plump pink submission on show for all the world to see.

Enchantingly winsome, calmly imperious, or downright domineering, Circe is female sexuality triumphant. Few men can withstand the assault of untamed lust, and in Greek myth only Odysseus is not blinded by the radiance of Circe, the sun god's child. The story goes that Odysseus and his men were returning to Ithaca after the successful conclusion of the Trojan War. It took them ten years to reach their destination, and on the way they fell into all manner of strange adventures. On one of these adventures, Odysseus's exhausted men took refuge on the island of Aeaea, where they found Circe's house surrounded by all the men she had transformed into beasts. Circe herself was inside, singing softly as she wove a wondrous web. When she saw the strangers at her door, she plied them with delicious food and spiked their drinks with magical herbs. As they sat there soaking up her beauty, they drifted off into pigdom.

On his way to wrest his men from the enchantress's clutches, Odysseus met the god Hermes, who gave him a potion and advice about withstanding Circe's charms. If she waved her wand, he was to draw his sword and she would capitulate immediately. In other words, he was to offer the temptress even more in the way of sexual delight than she herself promised. In the game of temptation, the partner who provokes the most desire has the winning hand. But Hermes warned Odysseus that when he stood naked before her, she might try once more to trick him (even heroes worry about losing control when disrobed); therefore, before he laid down his sword, he must make her promise not to take advantage of his vulnerability. Odysseus did as the god instructed and won Circe over. Well satisfied, she freed Odysseus's men from her magic and gave Odysseus detailed instructions about how to avoid the many dangers that lay between him and home. Then she sent him off to complete his quest.

One of the secrets Circe imparted to Odysseus was how to experience the loveliness of the Sirens and survive. The Sirens were beautiful women who sat in a flowery meadow by the sea singing so delightfully that sailors were lured to their shores. As long as the Sirens were singing, the men who listened thought them lovely. It was only when their ships broke apart on the rocks and death was upon them that the sailors saw the Sirens as they really were: ugly hags above the waist and claw-footed birds below.

On the strength of Circe's advice, Odysseus chose to rely on physical restraints rather than on self-control. When his ship neared the promontory where the Sirens lay in wait, he plugged his sailors' ears with beeswax so they would be oblivious to their charms. Then he ordered his sailors to lash

where others had failed. In preparation for his journey, he kitted himself out with winged sandals, a helmet that would make him invisible, a sickle from Hermes with which to chop off the Gorgon's head, an enchanted pouch to hold the prize he hoped to win, and the bronze shield of Athena polished to a reflective luster. As Perseus neared the Gorgons' cave, he put on the magic helmet and disappeared. Once Perseus was invisible, he approached the sleeping Medusa walking backward, using Athena's highly polished shield as a mirror to check on his progress. When he got close enough, he chopped off the monster's head and put it into his pouch.

The Sirens drowned themselves after Odysseus passed by unharmed and Odysseus never saw them again, but Medusa and Perseus continued to have a relationship of sorts. When Perseus slashed off Medusa's head, the winged horse Pegasus and his twin brother, Chrysaor, sprang from her severed arteries. Although the offspring were Poseidon's legacy, their appearance at this moment suggests that more than Perseus's sword had penetrated the sweet flesh of the sleeping Gorgon. Satisfied with a job well done, Perseus took Medusa's head and kept it safe in his pouch: as long as it was hidden from view, it had no power. But when Perseus took it out, it still turned all who looked on it to stone.

When Perseus asked the giant Atlas for a place to stay on his journey through northern Africa after slaying Medusa, Atlas refused. He was afraid of Perseus because he had been told that a son of Zeus would steal the gold from a magical tree in his kingdom. He was worried that Perseus might be the criminal in question. Angry at being turned away, Perseus reached into his pouch, pulled out Medusa's head, and turned Atlas into the range of mountains that stretch from present-day Morocco to Tunisia.

Perseus then continued his journey, heading to Ethiopia, where he spied a naked beauty chained to a rock by the side of the ocean. He discovered that she was a princess who had been left to appease a sea monster because her mother had angered Poseidon. Perseus freed the helpless creature and took her for his bride.

While Perseus was sitting down on the seashore with his new love, he was touchingly solicitous about the comfort and welfare of the severed head he had been carrying around with him for so long. Worried that the sand might irritate the writhing snakes on Medusa's head, Perseus made a soft nest for it in seaweed and ferns. As the powers of the severed head leaked out into the seaweed, they hardened it, creating a beautiful garden of coral. Now that Perseus had finally settled down with a woman he loved, the sensuous beauty of the Gorgon could be seen once more as an agent of delight rather than as an agent of destruction.

Feelings about Medusa have always been ambivalent. Chroniclers have written about the power of her blood to both heal and destroy. The Romantics and the Decadents of nineteenth-century Europe were especially fascinated by the dichotomies she embraced. Was she beautiful or was she a monster? For them, she had both mystery and power, two elements that became important in their view of a temptress as a woman who could both enrapture and destroy.

UNLIKE THE EARLY rabbis and Christian fathers who circulated the tales of Lilith and Eve to warn men how important it was to keep women—and their own urges—strictly under control, the ancient Greeks believed that consorting with temptresses offered men both a thrill to set the pulse racing and, if the men were careful, the opportunity to emerge both satisfied and triumphant.

The ancient Hebrews and the early Christians were struggling to survive in the face of oppression. The Hebrews suffered long periods in exile in Egypt, and the early Christians were being fed to Roman lions. Both groups imposed strict rules on themselves and on their women to ensure their continued existence. The ancient Greeks, in contrast, were steadily becoming the dominant culture in their region. By the fifth century BCE Athens was a democracy, and every free man over the age of eighteen had a voice in how the city-state was run. This was a society in which men were supremely confident, and they conducted many of their affairs as though women did not even exist.

But even in classical Greece, when times got tough, the specter of women using sex for power was not completely vanquished. In 431 BCE, the Athenian commander Pericles made the unwise move of declaring war on Sparta, a neighboring and warlike city-state. The Peloponnesian War, which lasted almost thirty years, devastated the once-proud city. In 411 BCE, the Greek playwright Aristophanes wrote *Lysistrata*, a comedy set in those dark times. In the play, the women of Athens band together to force their men to sue for peace; for as long as their men continued to fight, they withheld from them the pleasures of sex. Needless to say, in the play, at least, the fighting did not last much longer. Even in the most male-dominated society, men remain aware that women can use sex to bring them to their knees.

Chapter 3

Cleopatra

Seduction is the art of suggestion. Some sensual triggers are commonly recognized—the honey-like smell of the genital secretions of the nocturnal Ethiopian civet; the brush of fingertips across the inner elbow; the seed-studded flesh of a fig on the tongue; the glimpse of pillowy curves under fabrics as insubstantial as mountain mist. But many triggers are rooted in cultural conditioning and personal history. They change as individuals age and as cultures embrace new values and ideals. There is one historical temptress so potent that her image constantly fragments and re-forms to accommodate the dreams and desires of the era, culture, or individual that conjures her. She is Cleopatra.

In a seventeenth-century image of Cleopatra by Bartolomeo Gennari, the queen leans back, her barely clothed body turned to the viewer's gaze so that he can mentally remove what little clothing is left. The fangs of a small snake have pierced the flesh of her left breast, injecting poison into her body. The once-powerful Egyptian queen is drifting off into death. In this intensely private moment, exposed to the voyeuristic gaze of the observer, she is his for the taking. The woman who was said to administer poisons to her male slaves to gauge the poisons' efficacy and to offer men one night of bliss before their execution in the morning can be possessed at the moment she breathes her last breath. What sweet revenge.

For nearly twenty years, from 51 to 30 BCE, Cleopatra plotted Egypt's course in the face of the potentially all-encompassing power of Rome. Just eighteen when she ascended her country's throne, she entered into alliances with the most powerful Romans of her day, increasing her country's wealth and power until she had almost restored Egypt's former glory. In the end, she was defeated by the one Roman general impervious to her charms and she chose to take her own life rather than become his prisoner.

The unspoken, the insinuated, the power of suggestion are all powerful weapons in the telling of Cleopatra's tale. She was in charge of a vastly wealthy and subservient but still-powerful country. Egypt was an enigma to the thoroughly westernized Roman mind. The pantheon of animal gods was unfathomable. The women were unnaturally powerful. The morals were suspect. Displays of wealth were lavish. The colors, smells, sights, and sounds were all unexpected and exotic.

The Romans were often caught off guard in this country that supposedly owed them allegiance. When Pompey the Great sailed to Alexandria in 48 BCE seeking the Egyptians' assistance, they chopped off his head. When Pompey's rival, Julius Caesar, flaunted his high Roman status in the teeming streets of the multiethnic capital four days later, crowds chased him until he was forced to take refuge in the royal palace.

Then there was Egypt's queen, whose brother and co-ruler Ptolemy XII had banished her from Alexandria and was intent on ruling the country on his own. One day, while Caesar was still enjoying the young Ptolemy's hos-

pitality, a rug trader arrived at the royal palace with a delivery. When he unrolled his Oriental masterpiece, a proud young woman—fiercely intelligent, well educated, and descended from Caesar's military inspiration, the Macedonian ruler Alexander the Great—calmly stepped out and knelt before Caesar. She was here to plead her case before the fifty-two-year-old Roman general, who was known to have a way with the ladies. Only in this case, it seems that the young lady had her way with him.

After Cleopatra's visit, Caesar banished Ptolemy from the palace and raised an army in Cleopatra's favor. Ptolemy drowned during the ensuing campaign and was replaced by another, younger brother as co-ruler. Thereafter, Cleopatra held sway in Egypt—and with Caesar, especially after treating him to an opulent voyage down the Nile to show off her riches. Caesar was suitably impressed, and Cleopatra was soon pregnant with his only son.

When Caesar returned to Rome, Cleopatra followed despite whisperings and mutterings about the exotic foreigner and the bastard boy. Caesar, who had a wife in Rome, kept Cleopatra in a lavish villa on the outskirts of the city. There she held court, disseminating ideas about the divinity of leaders

and, some believe, inciting Caesar to push for his own elevation. After Caesar's murder by disgruntled senators in 44 BCE, she fled, family in tow, her alliance with Rome on an unsteady footing as various factions battled for power.

Back in Egypt, the younger brother who had been appointed Cleopatra's co-ruler mysteriously disappeared and she ruled alone. Cleopatra, a Greek by descent, had learned the language of her people and now appeared to them in elaborate ceremonies as the goddess Isis, the mother of all creation. The country prospered. Cleopatra governed and raised her son until a Roman victor emerged. Two victors as it turned out: Mark Antony and Octavian, who agreed to divide the empire between them, with Octavian taking Rome and the West and Antony taking the East. Cleopatra prepared to forge a partnership with Caesar's successor.

From the outset Cleopatra had Antony's attention, since he needed Egypt's backing for an ambitious military campaign. He summoned the

facing page: By the nineteenth century, the idea of an *Arabian Nights*-like Cleopatra had a firm grip on the Western imagination. In this era of travel and conquest, the East was there to be penetrated. She obligingly reclined, waiting to be explored and possessed. JEAN AUGUSTE DOMINIQUE INGRES (1780–1867), *THE GRANDE ODALISQUE,* 1814.

Egyptian queen. Cleopatra's first move was to heighten anticipation by making Antony wait. When she finally sailed into the harbor at Tarsus, in what is now southern Turkey, Antony was in the main square waiting to receive her. But Cleopatra had no intention of leaving her boat, which she had carefully prepared with Antony's well-known taste for opulence in mind. Over the deck of gold billowed sails of royal purple. Silver oars dipped into the water to the melody of pipes and harps. Cleopatra, dressed as Aphrodite—the Greek goddess of beauty, fertility, and sexual love—reclined beneath a canopy of gold, where she was fanned by young boys costumed as little cupids. The boat was crewed by young maidens dressed as sea nymphs, who trimmed the sails and guided the rudder with deft feminine fingers. The whole boat was enveloped in a cloud of intoxicating perfume.

Word of Cleopatra's wondrous vessel soon spread, and the crowds that had been gathering around Antony in the main square began to trickle down to the waterfront to see the breathtaking scene for themselves. As Shakespeare wrote in his tragedy *Antony and Cleopatra:* "Antony, / Enthroned i' th' market-place, did sit alone, / Whistling to th' air." A skilled manipulator of public opinion, Cleopatra had engineered a situation in which Antony had no choice. If the ruler of the eastern part of the greatest empire in the world was going to meet Cleopatra, he was going to have to go to her.

It is usually the man who wines and dines the woman before bedding her, but on the boat in Tarsus, it was Cleopatra who laid on the feast. The arrangement was obviously to Antony's taste as he dallied with Cleopatra until he heard word that his wife, Fulvia, had failed in an attempted rebellion against Octavian. When Antony left his Egyptian queen's caresses to straighten things out at home, he found public opinion beginning to turn against him. How could he expect to indulge in such enjoyment when governing an empire?

Antony was fascinated by Cleopatra, the rumormongers whispered, because she could satisfy him in bed with moves that no Roman matron could imagine, much less execute. As long as Cleopatra drew breath, Octavian's lackeys declared, she would be fixated on sex. The poet Propertius called her a "prostitute queen" and suggested that she had sex with her slaves until she was completely worn out. Lucan, a second-century Roman poet, suggested that she hated any man who did not satisfy her lust. The recorders of Roman virtue and Egyptian debauchery declared that the men in Cleopatra's court were reduced to "withered eunuchs" by her outrageous demands. Antony's manliness and fitness as the leader of a military nation was, by implication, much reduced.

Because Cleopatra was wealthy, the story was she had time to devise sexual delights for her latest lover. The fact that Egypt was peaceful and well governed during Cleopatra's tenure was of little interest to the storytellers, who left her administrative competency out of their salacious tales. Adding details to stories about Cleopatra's tremendous wealth a century after her death, the Roman scholar Pliny wrote that she owned two jewels of enormous size and incomparable beauty—pearls developed within the briny, vulval lips of the oyster. One day, Cleopatra dissolved one of her trinkets in a

cup of vinegar, which she drank to show Antony that their loss meant nothing to her.

The pearl story sets Cleopatra apart: she can afford to disdain what others regard as precious. Men wonder what it would be like to be around a woman who can casually destroy those things they most fear losing. It is liberating to imagine being with someone who could toss away precious objects without a second thought. When everyday cares and concerns are blithely disregarded, a special private space can be constructed, an isolated bubble in which the aspects of life and personality usually repressed can rise to the surface, bringing with them unexpected delights.

When Antony left Cleopatra to settle the matter of Fulvia's failed rebellion, he stayed in Rome for three and a half years. While he was there, Fulvia died and he married Octavian's sister, Octavia, to patch up his foundering relationship with his co-ruler. During Antony's absence, Cleopatra ruled her kingdom and gave birth to twins fathered by him, Alexander Helios and Cleopatra Selene, named after the sun and the moon.

One of Antony's goals when he took over the eastern part of the Roman Empire was to conquer the Parthians, who held power in what is now Iran and Iraq. Antony wanted to conquer this territory to ensure that the Roman Empire would rival the empire of Alexander the Great in power and extent. The Parthian conquest had also been a dream of Caesar's, and if Antony pulled it off, he would make it clear to Rome that he was a worthy successor to his mentor and predecessor in Cleopatra's bed.

When all seemed relatively stable on the home front, Antony decided to resume his quest to conquer Parthia. With such an important military campaign in the offing, he needed Cleopatra more than ever and summoned her once he reached Antioch in Syria. The Egyptian queen came, but she struck a hard bargain. She would fulfill his request if he would hand over to her the land that she wanted to expand Egypt's power. He did.

Antony needed Egyptian grain and Egyptian manpower to build boats with the timber that grew in the lands he had granted to the queen, but Octavian gave the Romans to understand that Antony was giving away Roman territory because he could not resist Cleopatra's feminine charms. Octavian had reduced Cleopatra's astute political bargaining to the power of a sultry wiggle of the hips. And he led Romans to wonder who Antony was conquering all this new territory for: them or Cleopatra?

By reducing both Cleopatra and Antony in Roman eyes, Octavian was advancing his own cause. Cleopatra was doubly suspect because she was both a foreigner and a woman. Foreigners, Octavian assured his fellow Romans, have disgusting customs, unsophisticated religions, and suspect morals. Women, he continued, are pleasure-seeking deceivers who have no idea about what is important in the world; men like Antony, who enjoy the company of foreigners and allow themselves to be sidetracked by women, are inherently weak. The choice the Romans had to make, Octavian implied, was clear.

When Antony's Parthian campaign failed, Octavian laid the blame at Cleopatra's feet. Antony failed because he had lost precious time while unable to tear himself away from Cleopatra's bed. The real problem, however, was that Antony had miscalculated the weight of his siege equipment, which was too heavy for his army to move. His miscalculation was compounded by bad luck: a trusted ally turned traitor and a surprise attack severely diminished his army.

Antony also lost more men in retreat than he needed to because he insisted that the army keep going through Armenia in the dead of winter instead of stopping to rest. According to Octavian's propaganda machine, Antony insisted on continuing because he wanted to get back to his Egyptian queen. "It was," Plutarch later recorded, "as if he were no longer the master of his own judgement, but rather under the influence of some drug or magic spell." But it seems more likely that Antony didn't trust the king of Armenia and wanted his men to beat a retreat out of that potentially hostile country while they had the chance.

Antony limped back to Syria and sent for Cleopatra. She had just borne him another child and was slow in coming, perhaps because it looked to her as though yet another Roman savior was turning into a disappointment. Antony's wife, Octavia, also came to Syria with ships and supplies. Antony accepted the supplies but turned Octavia back. Antony had made his choice, deciding once and for all to pursue his dream of an eastern empire with the Egyptian queen. His treatment of his Roman wife was the last straw for his compatriots back home, and Octavian had no difficulty persuading them that they should back him instead when the inevitable showdown came.

Cleopatra and Antony's story culminated in the disastrous Battle of Actium. It had become clear that Octavian and Antony were going to resolve their differences like men—by fighting. Antony and Cleopatra had not attacked Octavian in Rome, even though he was scrambling to get together

enough funds to mount an army, because they knew that Cleopatra would never be accepted by the Roman people if she invaded their homeland. The couple waited for Octavian to come to them. Once they had defeated him, they would be able to enter Rome victorious and the Romans would have no choice but to accept Cleopatra.

Cleopatra had built her fleet and was committed to a naval battle. If Antony fought on land, he would have to do so without her help. If he did *facing page:* Early Hollywood filmmakers surely had a ball with the costumes for the 1917 silent film *Cleopatra,* which starred Theda Bara as the treacherous Egyptian queen. The studio publicists jumped on the bandwagon, claiming that the star's name was an anagram for "Arab death."

that, he might lose her as an ally, which he could not afford. He opted to fight at sea. Unfortunately for Antony and Cleopatra, the man in charge of Octavian's ships, Marcus Agrippa, was a master tactician. Hemmed in by Octavian's forces at Actium, the lovers decided that the best they could hope for was to evade Agrippa's ships and use Cleopatra's treasure to build another navy.

As the couple fled, the story arose that cowardly Cleopatra had abandoned brave Antony in his moment of need—sure proof for the righteous Romans that he had been a blind fool to put his trust in such a treacherous thing as woman. "And it was now that Antony revealed to all the world," Plutarch later recorded with glee, "that he was no longer guided by the motives of a commander, not of a brave man, nor indeed by his own judgement at all. He allowed himself to be dragged along after the woman, as if he had become a part of her flesh and must go wherever she led him. . . . He hurried after the woman who already ruined him and would soon complete his destruction."

After the Battle of Actium, Octavian came to Alexandria seeking money, as both Caesar and Antony had done before him. Unlike his Roman predecessors, however, he did not bed the Egyptian queen. He was not interested in alliance but in domination. Cleopatra shut herself up inside her well-fortified tomb for protection. Thinking that Cleopatra was dead, Antony stabbed himself. When Cleopatra heard what Antony had done, she had him lowered into her self-imposed prison, where he died in her arms. Then she poisoned herself with an asp smuggled in to her in a basket of figs, to avoid being subjected to humiliation by Octavian.

Octavian couldn't have written a better ending for his temptress tale if he had tried: the great but flawed hero is undone by his intemperate love for a woman. Unable to drag himself from her bed when he should have been leading his troops into battle, he loses the prize he most covets—Parthia. When he takes a stand against his mortal enemy, his lover is cowardly and deceitful, sailing off with her fleet and guaranteeing his defeat, even though she has promised to stand by him. In the end, both die by their own hands— proof that when a man relies on a wily woman, his fate is sealed.

After Octavian's time, stories about Cleopatra took on a life of their own. There was Pliny's story of the dissolved pearl, and Plutarch's descriptions of the sumptuous banquets the lovers indulged in. Not one but many meals were prepared so that no matter when they decided to eat, there would be a banquet awaiting them, cooked to perfection. Then, in the fourth century, the story arose that the queen had toyed with men's lives for her amusement.

Lurking at the back of many temptress tales is men's fear of losing their masculinity in the presence of overarching femininity. In the Egyptian court, it was tradition to employ eunuchs, a practice that was abhorrent to the Romans. Octavian played on Romans' distaste for emasculated men by implying that Cleopatra was responsible. That she had chosen as her mates first one powerful Roman and then another was proof enough that she was usurping the male prerogative of making the sexual choice. She had the power, Octavian suggested, to reduce men to mere shadows of their former selves.

The logical extension was that she not only stole from men their masculinity but took their lives as well. And sure enough, the tale arose that men lined up to sleep with her knowing full well that the night they experienced the ultimate in sexual bliss would be their last, as she would have them killed in the morning. This cold and calculating image of Cleopatra struck a

Hercules and Omphale

· ·

I F THERE WAS one thing that the ancient Romans hated, it was an emasculated male. Roman men won their glory by outwitting other men in military or oratorical combat, realms from which women were traditionally excluded. A man who came under a woman's thrall was an object of derision. To compare Cleopatra and Antony with Omphale and Hercules, as Octavian did as part of his propaganda campaign,

was to question Antony's fitness as a military leader. The irony was sweet because Antony himself had first drawn the comparison—although Antony was thinking of Hercules' might and military prowess rather than his humbling stay with the Lydian queen.

The story is that the god Hermes ordered that Hercules be sold to Queen Omphale of Lydia to be her slave for three years after he accidentally killed his friend Iphitus in a fit of rage. The enslavement of a Greek hero by a barbarian queen was an outrageous idea, and Hercules' servitude was depicted as a humiliating experience. The Greeks said that Omphale dressed herself in Hercules' lionskin robe and brandished his club, while Hercules wore women's clothes and spun yarn for his mistress.

There was no middle ground for the ancient, warring Romans. Either the men were on top or they weren't. The equal partnership envisioned by Mark Antony and Cleopatra just wasn't an option.

chord with the Victorians especially, as they were preparing for their own vision of fatal womanhood: the vamp.

Cleopatra is handed down to us as an example of a woman with a voracious sexual appetite, who, when she was not seducing powerful Romans, disposed of lovers as one might put out the morning trash. However, there is no historical evidence that she ever had any lovers other than Caesar and Antony, and she spent long years apart from both of them, governing her kingdom. Both of these Roman generals were notorious womanizers, yet it is Cleopatra who has been taken to task for sexual licentiousness. How fervently, it seems, do men hope that the temptress is out there just waiting to pounce.

CLEOPATRA'S STORY has potency because it was originally told when the Roman Empire was in turmoil and its future uncertain. Octavian, if he were to prevail, had to make a strong case for his vision of a firmly Roman empire in contrast to Mark Antony's vision for a partnership between East and West. The historical facts of Antony and Cleopatra's story played beautifully into his hands, demonstrating that men who followed the path of pleasure not only lacked moral fiber but were bad choices as military and political leaders. But because Mark Antony was a great Roman, Octavian had to make sure that he was not sidetracked by any common or garden tramp. If he succumbed to Cleopatra's charms it was because she, in turn, was a great temptress, a mistress of her art. Octavian's propaganda exceeded even his own wildest imaginings. In trying to paint a picture of a woman men should avoid at all costs, what he created was the image of a woman no man could banish from his mind.

Chapter 4

Mistresses

Octavian and later Roman commentators described Cleopatra as a devilish seductress who had no compunction about disposing of lovers when they were no longer of use to her. But when it comes to mistresses, Cleopatra was the exception rather than the rule. For much of the time between the fall of the Roman Empire and the beginning of the twentieth century, it was difficult, if not impossible, for women to live independently of their fathers or husbands or brothers. It was accepted that women provided men with home comforts and heirs, and men provided women with provisions and—the women hoped—protection. In times when men's superiority was accepted by both sexes as a fact of life, men conjured up visions of delightful temptresses whose purpose was to entertain, not destroy, their men.

Powerful men on the lookout for delightful temptresses did not have to look far. When women's options for advancement were limited, there were always those who hoped to better their station in life—and perhaps even gain some measure of political power—by trading on their beauty. If men were wealthy and powerful enough, they found themselves in the enviable position of having beautiful women line up to show them their charms. The more beautiful and dazzlingly witty a woman was, the more the man wanted her on his arm and in his bed as proof that he was a man who had arrived.

Choosing a mistress has always been the temptress game at its most diverting. The man can enjoy the woman's seductive advances, secure in the knowledge that, as her benefactor, he will be safe in her arms. Like any game, however, it has its risks. There have always been ambitious mistresses who pushed a little too hard and even began to take over from the men whose paramours they were supposed to be.

In seventh-century China, for instance, Wu Zhao worked her way up from being one of many concubines to becoming empress of China by charming the emperor. And when her husband was stricken with polio, she took over running the country, annexing neighboring Korea. After her husband died, she reigned alone for the next fifty years. Madame de Pompadour, mistress of French king Louis xv, was another woman who basked in the reflected glory of the man whose bed she warmed. She was notorious for controlling access to the king and for meddling in the nation's politics.

When mistresses assume what society considers to be too much power, anxiety levels rise and their reputations as seductresses are often used against them. Two mistresses who walked the fine line between danger and delight were Lord Horatio Nelson's mistress, Emma Hamilton, and the lover of King Ludwig I of Bavaria, Lola Montez.

Lady Emma Hamilton

In the 1700s, wealthy and powerful men kept wives for appearances and mistresses for amusement. Society tolerated, even expected, such arrangements

as long as the men were discreet. A mistress was an amusing plaything, a creature to be cosseted as long as she distracted her man from his cares and made him look good in the eyes of the world. The sexier the mistress, the more envious the man's friends. The man who sported a fair young temptress on his arm was demonstrating to his friends that he was a man of power and influence. She might wink at them, but she belonged to him. Mistresses who lost the bloom of youth or no longer excited the ardor of their gentlemen were often discarded—sometimes with small living allowances or parting presents, and sometimes without.

The girl who was to become Lady Emma Hamilton, mistress of the English naval hero Lord Horatio Nelson, was born in the English countryside in 1765. She was brought up by her grandmother while her widowed mother worked as a seamstress and in domestic service. Emma was well looked after and was blessed with an extraordinary beauty that animated her whole being.

Not much is known about Emma's early life, but it seems that in her early teens she was connected with the Temple of Aesculapius in London, a sort of sex spa that dealt in matters of youth, beauty, and fertility. The temple was popular with the fashionable set, especially with men on the lookout for mistresses. Emma is said to have posed among classical statues depicting Hygeia, the Greek goddess of health. Draped in flimsy veils, she was a lovely advertisement for the health-giving properties of the spa's cures.

At the age of sixteen, Emma became the mistress of Sir Harry Fetherstonhaugh, the master of Uppark, a handsome country house in the Sussex countryside. At Uppark, she is rumored to have entertained Sir Harry's friends by dancing naked on the dining room table. The young temptress was perhaps a little too enthusiastic about her role as a provider of pleasure, for she soon had a huge falling out with Sir Harry, possibly over the parentage of the child she was carrying. Whatever her offence, Sir Harry was so angry that he turned Emma out of Uppark without a penny.

After she was discarded by Sir Harry, a somewhat niggardly and humorless friend of his took Emma off the streets by taking her into his bed. Emma could not afford to be without a protector for she had no other occupation to fall back on and no money of her own. She resolved to put her dramatic abilities to good use in a more calculating fashion. To please the Honorable Charles Francis Greville, who was fifteen years her senior and acted even older than his age, Emma tempered her natural exuberance. Once, when the couple was out walking in a park where music was being played, Emma spontaneously burst into song and was rewarded with warm applause from surprised bystanders. Greville was furious. As soon as they got home, Emma rushed upstairs to change from her good dress into the plainest dress that she could find. She then got down on her knees to plead Greville's forgiveness. She instinctively knew that her petition would carry more weight if her words were appropriately accessorized.

While under Greville's protection, Emma began to work as an artist's model. She became a favorite of the English portrait painter George Romney, who often used her when working on classical subjects. There was something uninhibited about Emma that especially suited her for the role of mythological sprite. Men who had heavy responsibilities in the worlds of politics, business, and war found her bracing country freshness most invigorating.

After four years of living with Emma, Greville decided he needed to marry a woman who had a fortune to her name. In a businesslike manner, he set about finding someone to take his young mistress off his hands. He approached his uncle, Sir William Hamilton, the British ambassador to Naples. Sir William was twenty years older than Greville, a bachelor, and a collector of beautiful things. They agreed that Greville would send Emma to Naples for a trial period of six months. The elderly connoisseur waited in anticipation: "The prospect of possessing so delightful an object under my roof . . . certainly causes in me some pleasing sensations."

Emma was furious about being handed from nephew to uncle and threatened Greville that if he cast her off onto Sir William, she would see to it that she became more than Sir William's mistress—she would become his wife. Greville thought this highly unlikely (as did Sir William). Why ever would a man want to court scandal by marrying a woman with Emma's reputation?

One day, however, the lazy, pleasure-loving King Ferdinand of Naples came across Emma and a companion strolling in one of the city's parks. When the king dismissed Emma's companion and made her a proposition many women would have been more than pleased to accept, canny Emma demanded his request in writing. The king, somewhat taken aback, agreed. Emma then took the note to the queen, threw herself down before Her Majesty, and begged to be saved from the unwanted attentions of strange men in Neapolitan parks. She gave no hint that she knew who the gentleman was but the queen recognized her husband's handwriting immediately, as Emma knew she would.

Queen Maria Carolina and her husband had an arrangement: the queen would run their kingdom and the king would have his fun. The only condition was that the king would be discreet. Propositioning the pretty young mistress of the British ambassador was going too far, and the queen gave Sir William to understand that should he decide to marry Emma (to get her out of harm's way), then she would be happy to overlook Emma's past and welcome her into polite society. The queen's hints, combined with Emma's powers of persuasion, led to Sir William's proposal of marriage.

In Naples, the newly respectable Emma became famous for her "attitudes," immensely popular depictions of great classical moments. With just a few shawls and her innate flair for the dramatic, Emma could lead her audiences from despair to elation and into despair again as she became Iphigenia preparing to sacrifice her brother Orestes to Artemis, then beautiful Esther who interceded with her Persian husband Xerxes on behalf of the Jewish people, then the sorceress Medea tearing her own children apart.

This was certainly a step up from her depictions of the goddess Hygeia in the Temple of Aesculapius. In London the men had ogled. In Naples, great ladies were led away from her dramatic spectacles in tears. Goethe, who was touring Italy in the late 1780s and caught Emma's act, wrote: "[The spectator] sees what thousands of artists would have liked to express, realized before him in movements and surprising transformations—one pose follows another without a break. She knows how to arrange the folds of her veil to match each mood, and has a hundred ways of turning it into a headdress." Emma reveled in the attention. She also had a quick wit and had no trouble learning Italian and grasping the intricacies of Neapolitan society. She soon enjoyed the confidence of the powerful queen and hosted lavish, fun-filled parties.

At the time of Sir William's ambassadorship, England was at war with France and Naples was neutral in the conflict. When Captain Horatio Nelson's ships came sailing by looking for somewhere to top up supplies on their way to trounce the French at the Battle of the Nile, Emma prevailed upon Queen Maria Carolina to let them land in Naples. When the terrors that had swept France during the revolution threatened to engulf Naples, Emma stepped in to save the royal family. Together, she and Nelson engineered the family's escape in British ships across the sea to the island of Sicily.

On the crossing, a terrible storm blew up. Sir William locked himself in his cabin and threatened to blow his head off rather than drown. Queen Maria Carolina had hysterics, and the nurse who was supposed to be looking after the queen's children was prostrate with seasickness. Emma rushed around tending to people, buoying their spirits, and comforted the queen's youngest son, who suffered from convulsions brought on by seasickness. He drew his last breath cradled in her arms. Greville had been charmed by a country waif, Sir William by a devoted nurse to an aging man. What Nelson saw was a vigorous woman who was not afraid to roll up her sleeves and plunge into the fray.

Nelson was a married man, but his wife, Fanny, was not an obviously affectionate woman. Emma's uninhibited nature gave the naval officer permission to unlock his emotions. Whereas Nelson's letters to his wife had been exercises in restraint, his letters to Emma were outpourings of passion. In one, he wrote: "The Conqueror is become the Conquered." Nelson was to be completely Emma's until the day he died aboard his battleship *Victory* during the Battle of Trafalgar in 1805—the letter he began to her before the battle started left unfinished.

After transporting the royal family safely to Sicily, Nelson was sent back to Naples to restore order after the terrors. Emma accompanied him as his personal secretary and interpreter. Nelson had to be uncharacteristically

bloodthirsty in dealing with the rebels, and Emma was variously depicted in cartoons in the British press as a gambler who frittered away Nelson's money during long nights of card playing and a Circe who had turned the noble British warrior into a pig. The feisty Emma did not help matters when she turned up at a fashionable fancy-dress ball in a state of near-undress as "the favorite of the harem." Both Emma and Nelson were relieved when Sir William decided to resign his position as ambassador and return to England. From then on, Emma and Nelson would be able to continue their affair on more familiar ground.

Emma was acutely aware that she owed her position in society to her husband, and Emma and Nelson were both solicitous of Sir William's feelings. Even while they carried on their affair in England after Sir William's return, Emma continued to live as Sir William's wife. Emma and Sir William lived in London but were frequent visitors at Nelson's country estate. Emma decorated Nelson's country house with tributes to his prowess in battle, but she also had the weeds cleared out of the little river running through the grounds so that her elderly husband would have a place to indulge his passion of fishing. When Emma gave birth to Nelson's daughter, the child was whisked away when she was less than a week old to be brought up in a foster home. On the few occasions little Horatia visited, it was always on days when Sir William was not at home.

Vivien

· · · · ·

THERE IS the lingering fear that the woman embraced as mistress might one day master her lover. This fear was immortalized in the Arthurian tale of Merlin and his young protégée, Vivien. Merlin was adviser to King Arthur's father, Uther Pendragon, and to the fabled King Arthur himself. He was, it seems, invincible. That is, he was until the fair Vivien came along.

When Vivien was Merlin's pupil, she longed to learn all that her master knew. Merlin was aware that if he taught Vivien all his magic secrets, she would betray him. But when she pleaded with him and promised him that she would never turn against him, the old man gave in to her demands. The Victorian poet Alfred, Lord Tennyson imagines the wizard's thoughts at her cajoling: "You seemed that wave about to break upon me / And sweep me from my hold on the world." Merlin showed her how to master him—and then he waited. Sure enough, reciting the words that Merlin himself had taught her, she cast a spell that imprisoned him forever in a crystal cave.

Why did Merlin capitulate? Tennyson explains: "The pale blood of the wizard at her touch / Took gayer colours, like an opal warmed." She could reach deep inside him to awaken sensations he had only dreamt of experiencing. When her warmth penetrated him, her embrace was the only universe he cared to experience. Such is, and has always been, the power of the temptress.

At Nelson's country retreat, Emma put on lavish dinner parties for friends from town and invited members of Nelson's extended family to stay. She had grown accustomed to luxury and spent money like water, much to Nelson's dismay. He might have been a war hero, but he was not a wealthy man. When Sir William died (both Emma and Nelson were at his bedside), he left Emma only a small allowance, presumably because he thought that Nelson would be looking after her. After Nelson's death two years later, she was left almost destitute.

For the last ten years of her life, Emma lost the will to charm. Although she occasionally still threw a memorable party, she was generally deserted by her former allies. She had acquired the habit of spending, and now that she was on her own she found it hard to cut back. She served time in debtors' prison and spent her last days in the rather dreary French town of Calais, so drunk she could barely get up from her bed. All her possessions had been pawned to buy alcohol.

Lola Montez

It is a hot, dusty day in Berlin in the summer of 1843. Thirty thousand Prussian troops are parading before their king and his guest, the czar of Russia, in their brand new uniforms. Entry into the royal enclosure is by invitation only, and the fiery Spanish dancer Lola Montez, who has been performing in the city to mixed reviews, has definitely not been invited. She has, however, hired herself a fine riding horse for the occasion, and takes advantage of a security breach to slip into the off-limits enclosure.

As the police try to sort out who is allowed to be where, a riding whip cracks and the astonished Prussian gendarme who has hold of the bridle of

Lola's horse drops back, allowing Lola to slip back into forbidden territory. Yet another man who thought he could tell Lola how to behave has experienced her unequivocal rejection of male authority and the indomitable force of her will. Armed with striking looks, a rapier wit, and dark, flashing eyes, the Irish-born Lola Montez, who has by dint of hard work and unrepentant dissimulation reinvented herself as a Spaniard, is not a woman to be trifled with.

Lola was born with her fiery temperament. Even as a child, she was described by one of her teachers as "a little tigress." From the ages of two to six, she ran barefoot through the intoxicating colors, sounds, and smells of northern India, where her father was posted with the British army. At the age of six, she was sent back to England to be educated. She soaked up her studies but couldn't wait to experience a wider world. At the age of seventeen, she eloped with a visiting army officer thirteen years her senior, only to end up back in India, where he was stationed.

The adult Lola hated the restrictions of the British army garrison, and persuaded her husband to send her back to England. On the long journey home, she scandalized the other passengers by having a very public affair with another army officer. By the time she reached London, her reputation was ruined. Her husband divorced her, her lover left her, and she was on her own.

By now Lola was well aware of her power to fascinate men. She decided to accentuate her charms by learning to dance. And what better kind of dancing to express her untamable nature than flamenco? Cajoling funds out of male admirers, she made a trip to Andalusia, Spain, to learn her craft. When she returned to London, she was no longer an Irish divorcée, but the

life threatened to catch up with her. After the incident with the riding whip in Berlin, she danced her way through Poland (where she was shown the border for causing a political disturbance) and Russia (where, for some reason, she also made a precipitous exit); through a brief, electric liaison with Franz Liszt (he said that she was the most enchanting creature he had ever known); through a ill-fated affair in Paris with a prominent journalist who was shot to death in a duel; through an expulsion from Bonn for scandalous behavior; and, in 1847 at the age of twenty-seven, into the arms of the staid and sober sixty-year-old King Ludwig I of Bavaria. After meeting Lola—a meeting at which she obviously took some liberties with the facts of her life thus far—Ludwig wrote: "The sixty year old has awakened a passion in a beautiful . . . twenty-two-year old . . . her very first! I can compare myself to Vesuvius, which seemed burned out until it suddenly erupted once again."

Ludwig appreciated the sharp erotic exchanges he could have with Lola, who wore pieces of flannel close to her body to drench them with her odor so she could pass them on to Ludwig to sniff. He also had a thing for her tiny, dancing feet and liked to suck on her (preferably unwashed) toes. Except for a couple of occasions, however, she kept him physically at arm's length and stiff with desire for her.

Lola set herself up in Munich, where King Ludwig's money flowed freely through her fingers. None of his politicians could stand her ill-concealed parade of younger lovers or her incessant meddling in government affairs. A small band of students fervently championed her, which led to scandal, especially when she was reportedly knocked out cold one night by a chandelier. It seems the students, having drunk freely at Lola's expense, had stripped down to their long shirts and drawers and paraded her triumphantly around her

house, no one noticing until it was too late the sparkling, low-hanging crystal.

But Ludwig, a powerful man, appreciated a woman with a mind of her own. Lola was never intimidated by authority figures or by hostile crowds; indeed, they usually brought out the combative side of her nature. After one especially heated confrontation with King Ludwig, she chased him into the street outside her house, screaming insults for all she was worth. When an angry mob, exasperated by her imperious ways, laid siege to her house in Munich, she appeared on the balcony brandishing a knife and then toasted the protestors with a glass of champagne, provoking a volley of stones. Tempestuous emotion complemented her savage beauty, and one observer of the Munich riot wrote that "she was lovely despite her rage."

When Ludwig refused to banish Lola—and even promised to make her a Bavarian countess—the Bavarian people started to lose confidence in their king. In 1847, his cabinet resigned en masse in protest of her influence and in 1848, estranged from his people and increasingly uncertain of his power, he chose to abdicate rather than go back on his word to his mistress. Lola was forced to flee the city. "You were born to be my misfortune," Ludwig wrote in one of his many poems about Lola. "You were such a blinding, scorching light."

Ludwig was to join Lola, but their affair cooled after she left Munich. After an illegal marriage in London (her divorce from her first husband stipulated that she could not remarry while he was alive), she pursued her stage career in North America and Australia, progressing from dancing to acting, for which she had a natural talent. After witnessing one of her performances, a critic wrote: "Up to now we could never fathom how it was possible for her to achieve such limitless influence over King Ludwig, who otherwise was never mild and malleable. Now, since she worked her witchery before us on the stage, we are fully convinced that poor [Ludwig] could not have mounted any resistance." Eventually, Lola took up public speaking, lecturing on what she knew: love, beauty, fashion, gallantry, and bold women. She mesmerized not so much with substance as with style, delivering her witty comments in a voice of "liquid sweetness" that left audiences hanging on her every word.

In the summer of 1860, at the age of forty, Lola suffered a debilitating stroke. She fought back and by December she was walking with a cane. For a while it looked as though she might fully recover, but on January 17, 1861, she died. She was buried in a small cemetery in Brooklyn. Her old lover, Ludwig of Bavaria, mourned her passing. Despite all the troubles Lola had caused him, he had never been able to banish her from his thoughts.

MISTRESSES THRIVE when society is stable and men are firmly in power. If kept women quietly accept their dependence on their patrons, they are regarded as luxury items appended to the gentlemen's estates. However, if these women get ideas above their station, the temptress aspects of their natures are accentuated. They become seductresses who have ensnared otherwise noble men. Their futures become subject to the vagaries of public opinion and if their lovers die or lose interest, they are in danger of losing all they have worked so hard to attain.

Chapter 5

Subversive Seductresses

Lord Nelson stuck by his Emma even when political cartoonists were holding her up to public ridicule; Ludwig of Bavaria was so taken with Lola Montez that he was prepared to give up his crown for her. Both mistresses found men who gave them wealth and security that they would have been unable to find on their own, and both were sufficiently beguiling that they held on to their men even when public opinion turned against them. There were some women, however, who made their way in life with more independence—and less certain protection—from men while trading on their beauty. The women were often courtesans, high-class prostitutes who offered pleasant company as well as sex to a variety of paying customers.

At the end of the nineteenth century, many of these women made the transition from private to public entertainment. In the shimmering gaslight, actresses and dancers transformed themselves into whomever their audiences wanted them to be. Prior to World War I, Parisian society especially was alive with the sparkle, suggestion, and sexual energies of courtesans and dancers.

facing page: Salome was popular with artists at the beginning of the last century. She was, by turns, young and frivolous, mature and knowing, or cunning and evil. In this painting, she is a mere child, but the severed head reminds the viewer that even young girls can be lethal. EDOUARD TOUDOUZE (1848–1907), *SALOME TRIUMPHANT*, 1886.

Salome

At the Folies-Bergère and the Moulin Rouge, skirts were raised and petticoats displayed as troops of long-legged beauties kicked up their heels. Toulouse-Lautrec sketched the mesmerizing performance of American dancer Loïe Fuller, the "Fairy of Light," as she crossed the stage, her swirl of artfully lit veils dispersing aphrodisiacal perfumes into the crowd. Men came to sit back and have their senses assaulted with dazzling public performances that they hoped might lead to more intimate affairs.

Behind the flash and sizzle, however, there was a creeping sense of dread. In Paris in 1896, there was the first public performance of Oscar Wilde's one-act play, *Salome*. Written in French in 1893, the play had been banned in England for its erotic overtones. Wilde was following an explosion of interest in the biblical tease as men across Europe, disturbed by increasing demands from women for political and social rights, began to probe the past for examples of dangerous women. Salome was rapidly turning into one of their favorite examples of how women can make men lose their heads.

In 1886, the French painter Edouard Toudouze had painted *Salome Triumphant*. In this picture, a young girl of about twelve is sprawled indolently on an ornate seat spread with a tiger skin. Her right ankle is encircled by a heavy bracelet that looks too weighty for her girlish frame. A profusion of flowers crowns her head. Jewels flash on her fingers and bracelets coil around her arms. Her dress is coquettishly revealing; the long, gauzy skirt is parted by two bare legs draped carelessly across the chair. Her slender arms hide her budding breasts.

This is no voluptuous beauty—this is a little girl playing dress-up—but the look in her eyes and the carefully posed fingertip resting at the corner of

her mouth suggest that she is wise beyond her years. She has caught the naked desire in her stepfather's hungry stare. She is playing with her newfound power, turning the bauble over and over, watching it catch the light. It is such a pretty, sparkly thing that rolls so invitingly in her hands. For her this is a game of visual stimulation. Desire at a distance. A dance to awaken passions that are meant to be fulfilled when she has exited the stage.

In Oscar Wilde's play, Salome's mother, Herodias, arranges a night of entertainment at which Salome will dance. Meanwhile, John the Baptist, a prophet much admired by Zealots planning an insurrection against Rome, is locked up in the palace. The Roman governor, Herod Antipas, is intrigued by John, who is firm in his views and offers answers in this world of uncertainty; Herodias hates him because he has questioned the morality of her marriage to Herod—the brother of her first husband, who is still living. The stage is set for Salome to dance.

Wilde gives no hint of how the Dance of the Seven Veils is to be performed; the interpretation of his stage direction is left to the powers of the individual performer's imagination. Aubrey Beardsley, illustrator of one published version of the play, conjures up a lascivious-looking Salome with a curvaceous belly ready to embark on "the stomach dance." During the Salome craze that was soon to hit North America, vaudeville performers expanded the belly dancing or "hootchy kootchy" routines first popularized by a dancer called Little Egypt at the 1893 Chicago World's Fair. Fifteen years later, in 1907, when Richard Strauss's opera based on Wilde's play premiered in New York, seductive undulations and dropped veils became all the rage. By late summer 1908 no fewer than twenty-four Salomes were

wriggling their way across New York stages, paving the way for burlesque shows and the striptease artists who would follow in the thirties and forties.

Nothing quite focuses a man's attention like a striptease, whether performed under a spotlight to a mass of maleness in a dark, smoke-filled room or to an audience of one in intimate surroundings. The woman's body, its contours, and the suspense of which inch of flesh will be revealed next are all that matters. Movement and music obliterate all extraneous details, and as the woman dances, the rest of the world slips away like the silk stockings that lie discarded on the nightclub stage or bedroom floor.

When Salome sheds her clothes, revealing firm, young skin with its promise of womanhood to come, Herod feasts his eyes. As she sways before him, he can imagine his lips on her flesh, his tongue tasting her sweetness. As she dances, sparking his desire, he promises to fulfill hers. After all, what could she desire that he cannot afford to give? But Herodias stands behind her daughter whispering into her ear the prize she should seize: John the Baptist's head. Herod is dumbfounded, but he has given his word.

The severed head lies on a silver platter in the foreground of Toudouze's painting, but the precocious child ignores the gory results of her request, oblivious to the historical weight of the moment. All she is interested in is seeing whether she can enrapture the viewer with her gaze as she has just enraptured Herod.

Mata Hari

In the Victorian age, men had begun to lose their complacency about their pre-eminent position in the world. Recent lessons in economics ushered in by the Industrial Revolution had showed them that fortunes can quickly be made and lost. The old hierarchical structure of society was creaking at the seams as the result of the unexpected pressures being put upon it. If merchants could become millionaires and gentry could let millions slip through their fingers, what standards were to be used to measure the worth of a man?

In concert with the economic changes, women were beginning to organize in unprecedented ways. In 1792, Mary Wollstonecraft had written a public appeal, *A Vindication of the Rights of Woman,* that argued for more autonomy for women. By 1848, a group of women had organized a women's rights convention at Seneca Falls, New York. In the Declaration of Sentiments arising from that meeting, they stated that "because women do feel themselves aggrieved, oppressed, and fraudulently deprived of their most sacred rights, we insist that they have immediate admission to all the rights and privileges which belong to them as citizens of the United States." One of their resolutions called on women to secure the right to vote. Fifty years later, British suffragettes would be throwing themselves under horses and chaining themselves to the railings of Buckingham Palace to get men to heed their demands.

There was a growing tension in men's minds between "women as men wanted them to be" (chaste, virtuous, and safely at home) and "women as men feared they might become" (insatiable, evil, and predatory). Left to their own devices, were all women going to become Salomes and shed their clothes before making outrageous demands?

Men nervously leafed through their Bibles and came up with long list of alarming precedents: Judith who cut off the head of Holofernes while he was sleeping, Delilah who robbed Samson of his strength before delivering him to the Philistines. Greek mythology wasn't much better: treacherous Helen

Delilah

. . . . . .

IN 1894, the French artist Paul-Albert Rouffio painted *Samson et Dalila*. The magnificently naked body of the sleeping Samson takes up the foreground of the picture. His head is tilted back onto Delilah's lap. His throat is exposed, and his long dark locks tumble down across Delilah's naked thighs and onto the bed. Samson is, at this instant, completely spent. His mind is floating on a last dying ripple of pleasure, and there is no room in this vast satisfaction for any thought at all. Today, all is especially dark, since Delilah has drugged his wine. Over her unconscious lover's head, she reaches for the scissors.

Delilah, planted by the Philistines to learn the secret of Samson's strength, has slowly but surely worn the strongman down. At first he teased her when she asked him the secret of his strength, suggesting various sources of his power, all of which were proven false. But when she threatened to withhold the pleasures of sex, he broke down and confessed that if his hair were ever cut, his superhuman strength would leave him.

After Samson was shorn of his locks, Delilah summoned the Philistines, who bound him and put out his eyes. Eager to show off their hard-won prize, they displayed him in a brand-new temple before a jeering crowd. Samson asked the boy who had led him in to guide his hands to the marble pillars on either side of where he stood. As he leaned against the cool stone, he prayed to God for strength and then pushed with all his might. The temple came tumbling down. Samson had one last moment of glory, but those who recorded Delilah's tale were eager to remind men that in times of war and oppression women can be especially treacherous.

whose beauty launched the Trojan War. Even British legend was not immune: the devious Morgan Le Fay who deceived King Arthur, Vivien who imprisoned the wizard Merlin in a crystal cave, mermaids who wrapped sailors in their arms and dragged them to the bottom of the sea. The Pre-Raphaelites, Symbolists, and Decadents painted these threatening women over and over again as men tried to decide if they were figures of the past or premonitions of things to come.

Into this increasingly swirling pool of turn-of-the-century paranoia stepped one independent young woman who had chosen to make her way in the world on the strength of her exotic looks and gorgeous body: Margaretha Geertruida Zelle, later Mata Hari. The Dutch-born beauty lost her comfortable middle-class life when her father plunged into bankruptcy and left the family when she was thirteen. Her mother died a year later, leaving Margaretha to fend for herself. She seems to have decided then and there to rely on her physical charms as, at the age of fifteen, she was dismissed from her training program as a kindergarten teacher for having an affair with the principal. At eighteen, she responded to a newspaper advertisement placed by a Dutch army officer looking for a wife. Thirty-nine-year-old Rudolph MacLeod was entranced by Margaretha's exotic looks and overtly sexual character. Unafraid of adventure, she plunged into marriage just four months later.

After Rudolph's extended home leave, the couple, a young son in tow, left Europe for an army post in the steaming forests of the Dutch East Indies, where all did not go well. The seductive features that had so intrigued MacLeod in a potential mate soon enraged him in a wife. MacLeod began to drink and abuse Margaretha. He wanted her to stay at home, unobtrusively mothering her son and new baby girl. Her dark beauty and vivacious personality, however, kept catching the young officers' attention. The last straw for the marriage came when a soldier with a grievance against the imperious MacLeod orchestrated the poisoning of the couple's two young children. The son died, but the daughter, Non, survived.

Margaretha was relieved when MacLeod was finally posted back to Holland, and as soon as the couple returned she filed for divorce. At the age of twenty-six, she was going to do the unimaginable for most women of her time—she was going to try to make it on her own. MacLeod, furious about his wife's waywardness, seized custody of Non, and Margaretha never saw her daughter again.

With little cash and no obviously marketable skills, Margaretha turned to exotic dancing. Drawing on her knowledge of Javanese culture, she re-created herself as the temple dancer Mata Hari, which means "eye of the dawn" in Malay. The fashionable set was mad for the East, and Mata Hari fed back to them their fantasies. One observer commented that her performances were like "an eternal desire for we-know-not-what offered to we-know-not-whom," and Frances Keyzer, reporting for the London society magazine *The King*, wrote:

> Vague rumours had reached me of a woman from the Far East, a native of Java, wife of an officer, who had come to Europe, laden with perfumes and jewels, to introduce some of the richness of the Oriental colour and life into the satiated society of European cities; of veils encircling and discarded, of the development of passion as the fruits of the soil, of a burst of fresh, free life, of Nature in all its strength untrammelled by civilization.

Mata Hari made her debut in 1905 at a fashionable salon in Paris. To the strains of Eastern music, she gradually removed veil after veil until, clad in nothing but a flesh-colored body stocking and jewel-encrusted breastplates, she collapsed onto the ground, prostrate before the image of the temple deity. For a woman to reveal so much in private was unusual; for her to do so in public was astounding. Mata Hari, however, had carefully calculated just how far she could go without being considered outrageous, and her dance was interpreted as tasteful cultural expression rather than as degrading smut.

On the strength of her debut, Mata Hari was called upon to dance at the Museum of Oriental Art in Paris, which gave her performance an anthropological stamp of approval. That same year, she appeared at numerous venues in Paris and soon rose to the top of her profession. For a decade, Mata Hari revealed the secrets of the East to audiences across Europe at such venues as the Monte Carlo Opera, La Scala in Milan, and the Secession Art Hall in Vienna.

Offstage, Mata Hari gave interviews that fueled her on-stage mystique. Margaretha transferred her personal experience of violence to the persona of Mata Hari as she fleshed out the details of life in the East for her credulous admirers. The Western mindset that had eagerly constructed stories of Cleopatra, the murderous "other," now soaked up Mata Hari's tales of a sun-drenched country where women were whipped for acknowledging their sexuality. The connection Mata Hari made between her performances and the breaking of sexual taboos drew audiences that could delight in the forbidden.

As Mata Hari approached forty, her marquee value declined and she relied increasingly on wealthy gentlemen to keep her in the extravagant style to which she had become accustomed. Courtesans were an accepted element of Parisian society and often wielded considerable political and social influence. By joining their ranks, Mata Hari could generate the income she required without sacrificing her independence. With characteristic vigor, she made conquests of powerful military men from nearly every country that was soon to be embroiled in World War I. She included among her lovers General Messimy, the French minister of war; Berlin's chief of police, Griebel; Baron Fredi Lazarini, an Austrian cavalry officer; and the Crown Prince of Germany.

When the war broke out in 1914, Mata Hari was in Berlin. Considered a resident of France, she was asked to leave immediately and many of her assets in Germany were frozen. She made it safely back to Holland, where she was bored to tears. She was desperate to get back to Paris, the site of her greatest triumphs. To get there in wartime, she first had to travel to England, where she was temporarily detained as British intelligence suspected her of being a German spy. She returned to Holland but finally made her way to Paris in 1916, this time via Madrid. On the strength of British suspicions about her, she was initially denied entry into France and had to pull a few strings to get herself across the border.

Alerted by the British to her questionable status, Captain Georges Ladoux, head of the French espionage agency, had Mata Hari followed for six months in Paris in the summer of 1916. Nothing came from this surveillance, however, except the discovery that she had an inordinate number of lovers, most of them military men. French, Italian, Irish, Scottish, Belgian, Russian—she enjoyed them all.

Then Mata Hari fell in love with a Russian officer young enough to be her son. She later swore that she "would have gone through fire" for him.

What she needed now was money—a lot of it—so that she could give up her life as a courtesan and support her young lover, the twenty-one-year-old captain Vladimir de Masloff. Ladoux made his move. If Mata Hari agreed to spy for France, she would get the cash payment she so desperately desired.

Mata Hari suggested an ambitious plan. She would get an introduction to General Moritz Ferdinand von Bissing, the officer in command of the German occupation of Belgium, and use this connection to reintroduce herself to the German crown prince who had once been her lover. Thrilled by the mission, she petitioned Ladoux—via regular mail—for an advance in order to buy a wardrobe suitable for seduction and set out for Belgium via England.

On her arrival in England, Mata Hari was once again detained. Sir Basil Thomson, assistant metropolitan police commissioner at Scotland Yard, later wrote that he thoroughly enjoyed interrogating her and was impressed by her lively wit. Mata Hari, meanwhile, elaborated on her fictitious Eastern connections and claimed to be involved in a number of espionage activities for the Allies. When Thomson contacted Ladoux to verify her story, Ladoux cabled back that he knew nothing of Mata Hari's activities and she should be returned to Spain. Perhaps he thought that if she really was a German agent, as the British suspected, she would tip her hand there. Thomson accordingly denied Mata Hari permission to travel to Holland, and sent her, along with her ten pieces of luggage, to Spain.

Undaunted that the British had thwarted her original plan and still eager to earn her reward from the French, Mata Hari set her sights on the conquest of the German envoy in Madrid, Major Arnold von Kalle. The investigative work that led her to him was simple: she looked up his name in the phone book, requested an appointment, and set to work. She coyly described her technique: "I did what a woman does in such circumstances where she wants to make a conquest of a gentleman, and I soon realized that von Kalle was mine."

Unfortunately for Mata Hari, von Kalle suspected her motives and decided to send messages to Germany about her in a code he knew the Allies had broken. If she was working for the French, these messages would make them believe she was working for him as well. The ploy worked. The French, anxious to crack down on spies to boost morale in their ravaged country, hauled Mata Hari in. The dancer-cum-courtesan-cum-amateur spy could not believe it. She protested vehemently that the only spying she had done had been for France. The French authorities needed a scapegoat, however, and Mata Hari fit the bill perfectly.

Sexy and unnervingly independent, she was definitely the kind of woman it was dangerous to have around. The stage had proved to be a place of liberation for many women in the early twentieth century, but when the war came, actresses and dancers, who often supplemented their incomes as mistresses and courtesans, were looked down on as subversive forces likely to upset the order of the world. Women feted for their performances when all was right with the world were now highly suspect. They not only ignored the rules but were privy to the most intimate thoughts and most unguarded moments of powerful men. If they slept with men for money, these self-centered, subversive creatures were also likely to sleep with them for secrets. The more erotic the woman, the more havoc she could wreak. And Mata Hari, a woman to whom borders meant nothing, was eroticism personified. She had to be stopped.

On 13 February 1917, Mata Hari was arrested on charges of espionage and taken to the Saint-Lazare prison for women. When Mata Hari had choreographed her dance performances, she had skillfully woven into her persona hints of temptresses past, such as the forbidden Oriental delights of Cleopatra. When times were good, such associations had served to heighten her appeal, but in the atmosphere of suspicion and intrigue of the war, associations with the exotic "other" now conjured up images of treachery rather than pleasure. Mata Hari's dark complexion, which previously had intrigued, now disgusted. Given the kind of woman she was, Lieutenant André Mornet, the prosecuting attorney for the Third Council of War in France, explained why she had to be guilty:

The Zelle lady appeared to us as one of those international women—the word is her own—who have become so dangerous since the hostilities. The ease with which she expresses herself in several languages, especially French, her numerous relations, her subtle ways, her aplomb, her remarkable intelligence, her immorality, congenital or acquired, all contributed to make her a suspect.

The media quickly made the connection between Mata Hari and the images of evil women that had been hanging in galleries and fleshed out in literature over the past fifty years just waiting for a moment such as this. She was described as "a sinister Salome, who played with the heads of our soldiers in front of the German Herod." She was compared to Delilah, another expert in getting men to spill deadly secrets. Her frank sexuality was cited as proof of her capacity for betrayal.

Gustave Steinhauer, a German spymaster, wrote that women became spies because of their lust for excitement. Whereas the male spy worked for the good of his country, the female spy was focused on self-gratification. And because of their inherently treacherous natures, women who turned to espionage were "far more cunning, far more adroit . . . than the most accomplished masculine spy." A novel based on Mata Hari's story emphasizes the intense personal satisfaction a woman derives from betrayal when the central character exclaims: "How I would fasten my mouth against their hearts! And I would suck them—I would suck them until there wasn't a drop of blood left, tossing away their empty carcasses." Appalled, those responsible for keeping order in times of mass destruction closed ranks against the independent international woman and had her shot.

Mata Hari was a sexual adventuress who had the temerity to assert herself in areas of male privilege. She herself had sketched the details that would ensure her destruction. She had portrayed herself as a woman without borders, a woman with an exotic past who reveled in the delights of sex. As long as peace reigned in Europe, such a woman drew crowds anxious to experience a vicarious thrill. When war broke out, however, men knew from all they had read and heard that a woman of Mata Hari's type was deadly.

The French prosecutors in Mata Hari's case rushed through the formalities to ensure that justice was done. The jury was swept along on the coattails of their conviction, even though, as the prosecutors later admitted, there was not enough evidence against Mata Hari "to whip a cat." The temptress mantle she had draped so coquettishly around her shoulders proved to be too effective a costume. The French firing squad believed it was doing its God-given duty when it reduced this vital and proud woman, who had brought so much pleasure to so many men, to nothing more than a "crumpled heap of petticoats," stripped of all their menacing power.

THE STORYTELLERS warn that when men are enraptured by women such as Salome and Delilah, they make wild promises and whisper secrets that contain the seeds of their undoing. Subversive temptresses of this ilk are so firmly entrenched in the collective male imagination that the image is easily transferred to real-life women who may—or may not—harbor the destructive, chaotic tendencies men are so quick to ascribe to them. An unfortunate few, like Mata Hari, find that the wave of male desire that sweeps them to success when the future looks bright turns into an undertow of male suspicion that drags them down when the tide turns.

Chapter 6

The Vamp

While Mata Hari's story was unfolding in Europe, another, similar, image of deadly womanhood was taking shape in North America. The North American image had its origins in European Romantic poetry and imagination.

As women began asking for more autonomy in the eighteenth century, men responded by suggesting that too much mental activity was bad for the female brain, and they encouraged their women to stay at home. A woman's worth, Victorian men decided, was to be measured not by her hard work or intelligence but by her virtue. The ideal woman was no longer the partner who toiled with her husband in the family business, but the household saint who sacrificed everything for her family. She would provide her man with a restful haven he could retreat to. When this virtuous lily submitted to sex, it was not because she enjoyed it, it was because it was her duty. Confined to genteel drawing rooms, women became interestingly pale and given to attacks of "the vapors." Men meanwhile lived their business lives in a cutthroat world of financial opportunism and turned increasingly to prostitutes for physical gratification. The gulf between the sexes widened.

In 1857, Baudelaire wrote "Metamorphoses of the Vampire," a poem about a woman who, after draining her lover of his "very marrow," dissolved into a putrefying mass, her true nature revealed. In 1897, Bram Stoker created Dracula, a male vampire who preyed upon women, who, in turn, drained the life from the men who loved them. The harder the Victorians tried to banish sex from their domestic lives—by covering up piano legs, and suggesting that mothers should not have sex for pleasure but only to produce offspring—the deadlier the portrayals of unrepressed sexuality.

While Stoker was creating Dracula, Philip Burne-Jones created an image of a pale woman with long dark hair clad only in a nightgown in a predatory pose above the sleeping—or possibly dead—body of her young male lover. He called his painting *The Vampire*. The Victorian writer Rudyard Kipling, inspired by the image, dashed off a poem of the same name. In part, it reads:

> A Fool there was and he made his prayer—
> (Even as you and I.)
> To a rag and a bone and a hank of hair—
> (We called her the woman who did not care)
> But the fool he called her his lady fair—
> (Even as you and I.)

Kipling explains how the vampire in the poem deprived her lover of all that he held dear:

> The Fool was stripped to his foolish hide—
> (Even as you and I.)

following page: By the time Hollywood got its hands on the image of the predatory woman, the man's fate was spelled out in vivid, chilling detail. In this publicity shot for the 1915 movie *A Fool There Was,* Theda Bara crouches over the skeletal remains of one of her victims.

Which she might have seen when she threw him aside—
(But it isn't on record the lady tried)
So some of him lived but the most of him died—
(Even as you and I.)

Here is the deadly temptress in all her glory. Cold, self-centered, and ruthless, she strips the man of everything and then discards him. Victorian men had backed themselves into a corner. They had turned their women into decorative accessories to be admired from a distance. They had taken them out of the bustling world of commerce and active social interaction and consigned them to the dark interiors of overstuffed drawing rooms. They had forbidden wives the delights of sex so that husbands could draw strength from an endless supply of virtue in the comfort of their own homes. Now these cold, pale beings were exacting their revenge. The goddess who was supposed to reflect the masculinity and success of her man was devolving into a bottomless pit of desire. She was climbing down off her pedestal. She was advancing on her man, closing the gap between them, and when she reached out her hand it was not to caress his cheek and murmur softly into his ear, but to rip the soul she was supposed to be nurturing right out of his body. Too extreme in its conception, the dream had turned into a nightmare.

A Fool There Was

In 1909, a play by Porter Emerson Browne based on Kipling's poem was a hit on Broadway in New York. Entitled *A Fool There Was,* it followed the downward trajectory of a privileged but weak male who could not resist the

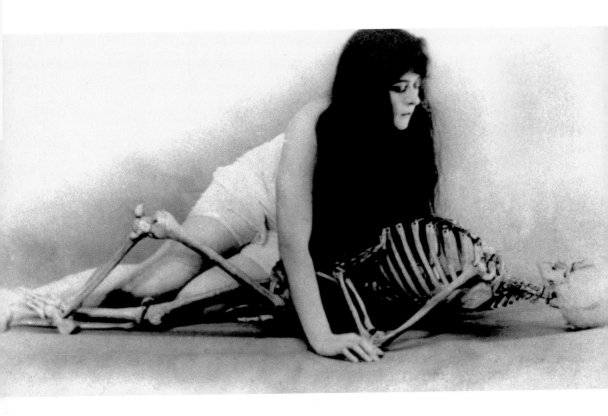

hypnotic gaze and rampant sexuality of a nameless, raven-haired woman. She had only to look in his direction and his mind turned to mush. He would abandon everything for her: his loving and virtuous wife, his beautiful young daughter, his successful business empire. No virginal lily she, this vampire was a blood-red rose with pungent odor to cloy the senses. She was the new Eve, the revived Cleopatra, the reinvigorated Salome, all rolled into one. She was mindlessly destructive of everything the man had worked so hard to achieve.

In 1915, Hollywood turned Porter Emerson Browne's play into a movie starring Theodosia Goodman, otherwise known as Theda Bara, or "the vamp." Pale and voluptuous, her dark eyes rimmed with kohl, Bara posed for publicity stills above a victim so drained of his life essence that only his bones were left. In the movie, it is clear that the effect of her kisses is not to invigorate but to deplete. She has clawed her way up from a murky background by means of her intense sexual magnetism. No matter how much she gets, it is never enough. Once she is through with one man and he has nothing more to

give, she moves on. She is unstoppable. She completely ignores the frail, virtuous woman at her victim's side because she knows the little wife does not stand a chance in the face of the vamp's voracious sexuality.

The kisses that Bara meted out in the movie were intensely physical and erotic. The camera positively wallowed in them. The male who had tried to banish sex from his everyday life was reclaiming territory with a vengeance. Now he couldn't escape urgent, violent sex. It was being forced upon him. He could take no responsibility for this bursting of the dam. She was fleshy and she was strong. He could practically disappear inside her. It was intensely satisfying and deliciously horrifying at the same time.

For all her intensity—in fact, because of it—Bara's vamp had a limited shelf life. Once the initial shock had thrilled through the system, even her most ardent fans could see that she was over the top. Her image, however, had such a hold on the male imagination that it did not disappear; it merely transformed itself, by World War II, into the femme fatale. One step in this transformation was the character of Lola Lola, played by the androgynous and sophisticated German actress Marlene Dietrich in the 1930 movie *The Blue Angel*.

The Blue Angel

In *The Blue Angel*, the vamp shed her voluptuous curves, and her husky voice—heard for the first time in the talkies—had a masculine cadence. Although she retained her ability to fascinate, and to destroy, this temptress did not roam the planet snatching any male she could find; she waited for men to come to her. And in this sense, the men who fell beneath her thrall were authors of their own demise. Strong men or men who stayed away were

Painted Ladies

. . . .

A T THE TURN of the twentieth century, the idea of the vamp had infiltrated Victorian society so thoroughly that even society ladies began to look fashionably evil. Portraitists took to painting the social elite staring out from the confines of sturdy gilt frames with a hooded, malignant gaze.

In this portait of the wife of a Scottish peer by John Singer Sargent, Lady Agnew sits with one arm draped over the side of her chair, completely at ease in the private space into which the viewer is intruding. There is an authoritative energy in the way she grasps the chair leg; she is relaxed but ready. All inside the frame is her domain. The viewer enters at his peril. Her right hand lies hidden in the folds of her skirt. Will she extend it in welcome or wait for the visitor to make the first move as she gazes up at him with those huge, unblinking eyes? She can afford to wait. The longer the suspended silence, the hotter under the collar the caller will become as he is forced to take the first step into the unknown.

This woman is not an object to be viewed but a subject in control. Just what kind of control she intends to exercise is unclear. The slightest trace of a smile suggests she might be planning some personal pleasure, possibly at the viewer's expense. She is confident that she will have no difficulty following through on whatever it is she has planned. The slightly cocked eyebrow both challenges the man to be up to the task of engaging with her and suggests her doubts that he will be.

In its extreme form, this preoccupation with the vamp led to legions of pale women, whose almost sepulchral appearance suggested they were connected with life on another plane. To add to her mystique in an age intrigued by the blood-sucking properties of women, the French actress Sarah Bernhardt (1844–1923) broadcast the fact that she took naps in a satin-lined coffin. The dancer Ida Rubinstein also promoted the look of a lean, clammy woman who might devour the world around her without adding so much as a touch of pink to her terminally pallid complexion. In *The Passing* (1911), her lover, American artist Romaine Brooks, painted her naked, laid out like an emaciated corpse on a coroner's table, her long black hair flowing to the floor.

safe. She affected only those of inherently weak dispositions who stepped into her lair. She was deadly, but she was also a sign that men were regaining their equilibrium—because only the weak succumbed.

When the film begins, Professor Rath (played by Emil Jannings), is an upright man of good standing in the community. As a teacher in a boys' high school, his job is to shape the characters and restrain the libidos of the next generation of manly leaders. Yet, when he pursues his errant charges to a nightclub, it is he who loses everything to the sultry star Lola Lola. Enthralled by a tantalizing glimpse of Lola's lacy lingerie after the show, the strict schoolteacher trades his personal fiefdom of the classroom for her world of the stage.

In his natural habitat, Rath is predictable, conscientious, and just a teensy bit dull. In her natural habitat, Lola Lola is the vessel into which men pour their desires. The good teacher inhabits a stable, narrow world; the sultry performer is constantly sweeping her ever-changing environment for her next mark. He deals in mind-improving classics; she deals in fantastic dreams. He is completely bewitched by a feminine nature that he does not understand but that he desperately wants to experience; she knows only too well how to make herself the focus of a man's attention.

Rath's lack of resistance is his downfall. Innocent of the ways of the world, he succumbs too easily to Lola's tawdry charms. Once he marries her, he becomes her lapdog. He fetches and carries for her, helping her transform herself into a vision of bewitching beauty for other men to feast their eyes on. She sends out come-hither looks to the men in the audience. They, like her husband, cannot resist. And Rath is powerless. He can do nothing as Lola slowly but surely drains him of his masculinity.

At the end of the movie is the ultimate humiliation. When Lola's troupe returns for a performance in Rath's hometown, he is paraded before his former students as a clown and a cuckold. Those over whom he once wielded authority double up with laughter when they witness the state to which he had been reduced.

This, by the 1930s, is the power of the vamp. Not only will she suck the life out of a man, she will make a fool of him in front of his peer group, the powerful males he must impress if he is going to keep his place in the world. Weak men cannot allow themselves to be sucked into the woman's realm, the movie suggests. They must keep themselves apart and engage in manly pursuits. The feminized man is an object of ridicule. Men who sympathize too closely with women in their quest for equality are being toyed with. They are weak fools. "Leave her bed. Come back to your drinking buddies," the other men proclaim. "She'll take you nowhere but down. Stick with us and we can give you the world."

LOLA LOLA kept the thread of the destructive temptress story alive until the creation of the femme fatale in the 1940s. In the meantime, another, less threatening temptress was in the making.

Chapter 7

The Bombshell

Mata Hari, the erotic spy, and Theda Bara, the vamp, were destructive temptresses created when upheaval in world events and women's agitation for rights coincided to seriously undermine men's confidence in the future. After World War I, life was good. Prosperity returned, especially in North America. The war had not brought the end of the world, as some had feared. Women remained helpful and supportive, and the traditional values of love and marriage seemed intact. Men rewarded women for their cooperation during the war years by granting many of them the right to vote. In Britain, after sixty-five years of politely asking for the vote and five years of angrily demanding it, women over thirty were finally allowed to participate in national elections. Most of Canada and Europe followed suit, and by 1920, women in the United States gained the same rights.

Allowing women to participate in democracy did not immediately lead to chaos, and men relaxed a little. And in the 1920s, the flapper emerged in North America. This vivacious young woman had shed her dangerous curves and left her sultry demeanor behind. With her bound breasts, bobbed hair, and short, straight skirts, she was positively boyish. Unlike the vamp, she had no master plan. She was fun. She was lively. She was eager to experiment.

In these good times, men no longer saw temptresses lurking on dark street corners waiting to pounce on the unwary. Life was bright and full of parties and too much alcohol. There was the occasional gold digger, to be sure, and the odd woman who was too insouciant with her emotional attachments—vestiges of the self-centered, coldhearted vamp—but the men were rich and could afford to keep attractive women who loved pretty things. Some women were sharp-witted and sharp-tongued, but there were enough party girls to balance it all out. By the 1930s in Hollywood, the predatory vamp of the teen years had been replaced by the exuberant bombshell. She was sex on the screen, a fantasy come true. She was as bright and bubbly as the vamp had been cold and sinister. And, unlike the dark, sultry vamp, she was dazzlingly, electrically blonde.

The epitome of this new delight was Jean Harlow, who, after the studio publicity machine was done with her, became known as the Platinum Blonde. Harlow had the looks for her seductive role even when she was a teenager. One future close friend described what happened when the teenage Harlean Carpenter came to her house after her father had invited some of his friends over to play cards: "The doorbell rang, and there was this *amazing* girl with white-blonde hair and gorgeous green eyes. The men just *stared*." Another said, "Even at that age [around sixteen], Harlean Carpenter was the most *gorgeous* creature I ever saw. Flawless skin; so fair she was almost albino. . . . She was only 5'2", but her figure was beautifully balanced. A great pair of legs, size three and a half feet, and a wonderful smile. . . . When we walked down the street, she would literally stop traffic. Men would climb out of their cars and follow her."

Little temptresses-in-the-making, it seems, just cannot help but look sexy, no matter what they are wearing. Harlow oozed sex, even in her elementary school days. "Miss Harlean Carpenter was unforgettable, even in the school uniform, which was seductive only on her. No middy blouse but hers was cut so low, and, despite admonitions, her hips swayed under the ankle-length pleated skirt." Harlow knew there was more to being beautiful than just standing there: there is nothing quite like sexuality in motion. A fellow student confirmed this by reporting her father's reaction on seeing Harlean at the school. The older man confided to his daughter: "They [the other pupils] all just walked . . . except Harlean—she sashayed."

Such fun kinds of temptresses take a wholesome enjoyment in the beauty of their bodies. Even in her early days in Hollywood, Harlow was perfectly comfortable with the effect her physical appearance had on others. In 1929, she was making the silent film *Double Whoopee* with Stan Laurel and Oliver Hardy. The scene called for Harlow's skirt to be shut in the door of a taxi by the clumsy doorman played by Laurel. As she stepped forward, her skirt was left behind. She then walked through the hotel lobby wearing nothing but a see-through slip, unaware that anything was amiss.

Someone had told Harlow that for this scene, she had to be "under-dressed." Still new to the world of film, she did not know that this meant she was to be wearing flesh-colored tights under her costume; she thought it meant wearing no underwear. The unself-conscious Harlow was happy to oblige. Actor Rolfe Sedan, who was playing the part of the hotel receptionist, reported: "We weren't told that she was going to come in naked. Nobody

knew. . . . When she came up to the desk, for a moment I almost didn't say the words."

When Harlow was asked to remove her jacket during filming of the 1932 movie *Red-Headed Woman*, she did not hesitate, even though she had absolutely nothing on underneath. "Nudity was rarely seen in those days, and Harlow's had the startling quality of an alabaster statue. Visitors on the set scarcely believed their eyes. The lighting crew almost fell out of the flies [high up where the scenery is stored] in shock."

Playful temptresses often take positive delight in exposing their charms. The 1932 movie *Red Dust* contained a scene where Harlow was bathing naked in a rain barrel. As the cameras rolled, she leapt up, exposing her bare breasts and exclaiming, "Something for the boys in the lab!" Director Victor Fleming yanked the film from the camera to make sure these shots of Harlow did not make it out of the studio. A sex symbol she might be, but there were limits to how far the studio could let her image go.

One of Harlow's most famous lines came in the 1930 movie *Hell's Angels*, directed by the eccentric Howard Hughes before he withdrew from the world. In this film, Harlow plays a sexually aggressive woman who smokes, drinks, and shows lots of that lovely alabaster skin. In one scene, after luring her latest suitor's brother into her apartment, she pours herself a drink as she takes off her wrap. "Would you be shocked if I put on something more comfortable?" she asks. The remark entered common parlance in a somewhat altered form: "Would you mind if I slipped into something more comfortable?" and became a classic opening line for any temptress.

Harlow was given roles that played up her reputation as a bad girl whom it might be dangerous to know, and she became notorious for having few qualms about displaying her body. She disdained underwear and often had to be sewn into her costumes. On the set of the 1931 movie *Iron Man*, actors and workers alike rushed to see her play a party scene in a see-through sheath. "She made her entrance down some steps, and as she did, everything under that dress kept coming out and going in! People were swarming from all over to see it," one witness said. Harlow had various tricks of the trade to show her skintight gowns off to best advantage. She was said to bleach her pubic hair so that it did not show through sheer, tight fabric, and on the set of the 1931 movie *The Public Enemy*, James Cagney, the co-star she was to seduce, was fascinated by her ever-perky nipples. Eventually, his curiosity got the better of him. "How do you hold those things up?" he asked. "I ice 'em," she replied.

A certain brazen quality often helps temptresses achieve their ends, and Harlow certainly showed this, even when she was not on a movie set. Playing up her image, she arrived at one Hollywood party in an especially low-cut gown. When her hostess remarked cattily, "Why, dear, that dress is down to your waist," Harlow calmly slipped her gown off her shoulders so

Clara Bow

· · · · · · · · ·

THE BOMBSHELL took shape as the silent movies gave way to the talkies. But there was one star who embraced sex and seduction who did not survive the transition to sound: Clara Bow, the "It" girl. As described by the Edwardian socialite turned Hollywood sex guru Elinor Glyn, "It" was a quality that drew the opposite sex the way sun-ripened fruit draws hungry wasps.

What distinguished Bow from the other stars of her day was the vital, almost manic quality to her acting. Producer Adolph Zukor wrote of Bow that "some part of her was always in motion, if only her great rolling eyes. It was an elemental magnetism, an animal vitality." Director Dorothy Arzner likened her to "a dancing flame on the screen." One of the reasons Bow never made it to the talkies in the days of fixed microphones was that she never stood still long enough for the sound crew to be able to position their recording equipment properly. She darted and dazzled, like a tiny humming-bird off to suck her next flower.

Offscreen, *Variety* magazine called her a mantrap, and a room in her house decorated in Oriental style was reportedly referred to as her "loving" room. When Gary Cooper was lured into this den of iniquity, all he could do was gulp and say, "Aw, gee." When one lover staged a dramatic suicide attempt complete with blood dripping down over a photograph of his beloved, Bow was unimpressed. "Lemme tell ya this," she told a reporter, "when a man attempts suicide over a woman, he don't cut his wrists with a safety razor blade, then drape himself over a couch with a cigarette between his lips. No, they don't do it that way. They use *pistols*."

The little jazz baby knew her days of first billing were numbered when newcomer Jean Harlow stepped onto the set of the 1929 movie *The Saturday Night Kid*. "[Harlow] was wearing this black-crocheted dress with *not a stitch* on under it. From where I sat, you couldn't tell whether she had put it on or *painted* it on," said the assistant director Artie Jacobson. Bow's reaction was instantaneous. "Who's gonna see me nexta her?" she snapped.

that it really was hanging around her waist. As usual, she was braless. "Could I have some more coffee?" she calmly asked the stunned hostess.

When Harlow was invited to a dinner party at millionaire William Randolph Hearst's 67,000-acre estate, Hearst thought what she was wearing looked more like a nightgown than an evening gown. He told his movie-star mistress, Marion Davies, to ask Harlow to get dressed. Harlow reluctantly left the table only to come back wearing an overcoat, which she wore for the duration of the meal as a silent rebuke to Hearst for his stuffiness.

Much of Harlow's screen work was designed by the male-dominated studios of her day to make the most of her sizzling sexual presence. Writer Graham Greene wrote that in her last movie, *Saratoga*, "She toted a breast like a man totes a gun." And when cameraman Leon Shamroy shot a screen test for another sex bomb, Marilyn Monroe, in 1946, he commented: "[Monroe] got sex on a piece of film like Jean Harlow."

The most delightful aspect of Harlow's screen sizzle was that it packed heat without inflicting a nasty burn. She might have been vigorous and feisty and happy to display her God-given charms, but she was also not averse to being slapped about a bit by hunky male stars like Clark Gable. Now, the males in the audience thought as they settled back into their seats, this is more like it.

FILM IS A PERFECT medium for reflecting temptress images. When the shift from vamp to bombshell played out during and after World War I, the chilling predator was replaced by a feisty woman who gave a man a delicious run for his money but capitulated in the end. There was a sense that the

bombshell, as played by Jean Harlow, enjoyed the skirmishes of the battle between the sexes, but underneath it all each side understood and accepted the other. And, most importantly, that each side knew the woman would knuckle under in the end.

The cycle of fatal to fluffy would be repeated in the years during and after World War II, with the arrival of the sultry femme fatale and her ultimate displacement by the adorable sex kitten as played by the fifties successor to Jean Harlow, Marilyn Monroe. In each circuit of their fears, men's anxiety rose as war threatened the stability of their lives and receded when their fears proved groundless. Once again, they were riding out self-induced storms of the psyche that buffeted and reformed their views of women, while women did their best to ride out the currents of desire.

facing page: Director Rouben Mamoulian said Rita Hayworth conveyed "an inner grace that cannot be acquired and [has] the additional lure of sending out some sort of vibrations, the lust of which audiences immediately sensed."

Chapter 8

The Femme Fatale

Unfortunately, the sparkling promise of the twenties was short-lived. Prolonged drought in North America and the stock-market crash on Wall Street that triggered the Great Depression of the thirties shattered men's confidence. To make things worse, by the early 1940s, another world war was looming. Men, well versed in stories of female treachery in times of unrest—Salome, Delilah, Mata Hari—began casting suspicious glances at women once again.

Male nervousness was compounded by the fact that women had proved themselves so capable during World War I. Women could be expected to step up to the plate once again, wielding wrenches, welding airplane parts, and organizing matters while the men were away at war. Only this time, they had the vote and had experienced the freedoms of the 1920s. Men were anxious about their livelihoods: when the soldiers came back from war, would women meekly set down their riveting guns and go back into the kitchen? What men wanted was reassurance. What they got was the femme fatale.

The femme fatale of the film noir of the 1940s was a sexual predator who used men as tools to get what she wanted. Unlike the meek little wife

Keep mum she's not so dumb!

CARELESS TALK COSTS LIVES

who equated sex with love and security, the femme fatale equated sex with power and ambition. This was a woman who could get a man to turn against his fellow men and carry out her dirty work for her. By dissecting her approach on screen, the filmmakers were giving men the key to freeing themselves from her influence— just in case the soldiers coming home from the war found her waiting on their doorsteps.

Mrs. Dietrichson

Marlene Dietrich's Lola Lola was the bridge between the vamp and the femme fatale. The vamp is an active predator, a tiger who actively stalks her victim, sinks her teeth into him, and bleeds him dry. Lola Lola is a shadowy lurker, a spider who waits for the fly to land on her sticky net so she can slowly but surely squeeze all the masculinity out of him. The femme fatale, in contrast, is a beautiful serpent whose devastating gaze hypnotizes her man into becoming the agent of his own destruction. The English Romantic poet John Keats outlined the type in his epic poem *Lamia,* which tells of a serpent that turns into a woman to seduce a mortal. He describes her charms:

> She was a gordian shape of dazzling hue,
> Vermilion-spotted, golden, green, and blue;

Striped like a zebra, freckled like a pard,
Eyed like a peacock, and all crimson barr'd; [. . .]
Upon her crest she wore a wannish fire
Sprinkled with stars, like Ariadne's tiar:
Her head was serpent, but ah, bitter-sweet!
She had a woman's mouth with all its pearls complete: [. . .]
Her throat was serpent, but the words she spake
Came, as through bubbling honey, for Love's sake, [. . .]

The Romantic poets of the nineteenth century had identified the "tempestuous loveliness of terror," and the filmmakers of 1940s Hollywood brought it to fruition in the femme fatale.

In the 1944 movie *Double Indemnity,* cool, blonde Barbara Stanwyck plays Mrs. Dietrichson, a serpentine, dissatisfied wife. Her successful husband offered her hope of wealth and social position, but he never delivered. Instead, he plows all his hard-earned money back into his business ventures, complaining loudly when his wife goes on a shopping spree. She will not even benefit when he dies: his life insurance policy is made out in the name of Lola, his daughter from a previous marriage.

One day insurance salesman Walter Neff (played by Fred MacMurray) knocks on the door to renew her husband's automobile policy. Neff is young, bright, and just a little too cocky. Mrs. Dietrichson has been waiting for such a moment as this, and she turns on the charm. The air in the drawing room instantly becomes electric. Sexual innuendoes fly back and forth between the salesman and the embittered wife. While Neff is savoring the tingle their conversation gives him, Mrs. Dietrichson is converting energy into action.

What would happen, she asks him sweetly, if she were to insure her husband's life and an accident were to befall him?

Like so many men who become embroiled with this particular brand of temptress, Neff is an expert in his field. He knows all about the insurance business; it is a game with clear-cut rules. Every once in a while a man tries to cheat, but it's not hard to smoke him out and set things right again. Insurance men are convivial and stick together, like an extended family. At work, Neff has respect and support. Life is good. And yet, this woman is throwing down a gauntlet, challenging him to fix her predicament. She entices him with flattery: "I suppose you have to think of everything in your business," she coos.

Neff's no fool and wants no part of her scheme. Why would he? But a temptress knows how to get under a man's skin. With the benefit of hindsight, the dupe ruefully observes, "I knew I had hold of a red hot poker and the time to drop it was before it burned my hand off." Needless to say, he held on—tight. She comes to his apartment, articulating what he doesn't dare: "You forgot your hat this afternoon. Don't you want me to bring it in?"

The femme fatale works on her victim on two levels. She awakens both his desire to bed a beautiful woman and his desire to outwit his male peers— intensely primal emotions that are capable of pushing the man to reflexive rather than reflective action. The man wants to enjoy the femme fatale's body, but he is also tempted by the idea of stepping up a rung on the male-defined ladder of success. Mrs. Dietrichson gives Neff an electric thrill, plus the opportunity to test his mettle against his boss.

Neff's boss, Barton Keyes (played by Edward G. Robinson), is the best in the business at sniffing out false insurance claims. Here is Neff's opportu-

nity to show how the student has surpassed the master. Mr. Dietrichson's murder will be his rite of passage, his ticket to the ranks of the truly extraordinary. Mrs. Dietrichson senses his ambition and uses it for her own ends. She gives him a chance to create chaos in his ordered world, to break off from the group and make his mark as an individual. He would never do that on his own, but she makes him feel invincible. Just like the Sirens who tried to waylay Odysseus, she is dangerous because she unleashes and feeds his deepest desires.

The idea is thrilling, but the reality—at least in the 1940s—is that such plans cannot succeed. In the film noir, the woman and the man she has tempted pay for their crimes, usually with their lives. This is the message to the men in the audience. You may want to throw off your responsibilities and try to make it alone. You may think you can defy convention and hook up with a woman who does not respect the rules. But don't do it. We, the other men, the ever-vigilant ones, will catch you and make you pay. It won't be worth it, we promise. And yet, the competitive instinct is hard for the tempted man to shake off. Who knows, perhaps if they planned well enough, they could get away with it and he could have that gorgeous woman all to himself in the end.

In *Double Indemnity*, Neff, using his insider's knowledge of the insurance business, plans the perfect murder. He and the seductive Mrs. Dietrichson are a team. They know the plan by heart. But carefully, patiently, Barton Keyes begins to tease out the strands of the story. He might never have figured out the answers, but in the end he doesn't need to because Neff and Mrs. Dietrichson become agents of their own destruction. The heart of the disintegration is the breakdown of trust between the perpetrators of the crime. When Neff sees his chance to pin the murder on another man, he visits Mrs. Dietrichson late at night planning to kill her. Once she realizes Neff will no longer stand by her, Mrs. Dietrichson makes a similar plan to get rid of Neff. They end up shooting each other, their passion turned sour.

Despite her dangerous aspect, the femme fatale is not as sinister as the vamp who preceded her. Whereas the vamp is unconstrained by the male world around her, the femme fatale operates within the confines of male-generated rules. The femme fatale does not act alone, as her earlier predatory sisters did. Despite men's fears, she cannot break free of her dependency. The focus of the film noir often becomes not the sexual attraction between the temptress and her victim but the chemistry between the two male protagonists. How will their struggle for supremacy play out? *Double Indemnity* is framed by the relationship between Neff and Keyes. Neff wants to prove that he can outwit Keyes, but Keyes demonstrates that it is dangerous for men to challenge the system that nurtures them—especially when beautiful women ask them, ever so nicely, to do so.

Most significantly, however, unlike Theda Bara's vampire of the teen years or Marlene Dietrich's Lola Lola of the 1930s, the femme fatale of the 1940s does not get away with her crime. At the end of the movie, the male-

The Sphinx

. . . .

THE SHADY motives of the femme fatale show how much of a riddle women are to men. If a man cannot figure out what a temptress is up to, he may be in grave danger. The enigmatic and treacherous nature of women is highlighted in the ancient Greek tale of the Sphinx that terrorized the city of Thebes before she was outwitted by the hero Oedipus.

The Sphinx is traditionally depicted as having the body of a lion, the wings of an eagle, and the breasts and face of a woman. She was the daughter of the venomous, fire-breathing Typhon and the beautiful, snaky Echidna. She sat on a rock near the gate to Thebes and challenged all who passed by to answer the question: "What has four legs in the morning, two legs at noon, and three in the evening?" She strangled anyone who could not answer. When Oedipus answered correctly, "Man," the Sphinx threw herself off her rock to her death.

From her parents, the Sphinx inherited physical beauty combined with deadly passion and serpentine wiles. In her physical attributes, she combined the destructive powers of both the sharp-clawed eagle and the predatory lion. She was a creature capable of targeting, stalking, and then destroying her chosen prey. Before dispatching them, however, she allowed herself the satisfaction of challenging them with her mind-twisting riddle. As the twentieth century progressed, the predatory vamp gave way to the scheming femme fatale, each image reflecting an aspect of the inscrutable Sphinx until the radiant aura of the sex kitten erased the Sphinx's sinister shadows in its rosy glow.

dominated system triumphs. The evil temptress has done her darndest to upset the system, but the forces of good have triumphed in the end. Men can come home from the war confident that the system has not fallen apart in their absence. They can enjoy watching the femme fatale weave her web, secure in the knowledge it can be broken. They can concentrate on the delights of her body rather than on the depredations of her mind. The wayward woman is well on her way to being tamed.

Gilda

No one projected the aura of the 1940s femme fatale quite like Rita Hayworth did with her title role in the 1946 film noir *Gilda*. The subject is a ménage à trois. On the one hand, there is the business relationship between a casino owner named Ballin Mundson (played by George Macready) and Johnny Farrell (played by Glenn Ford). On the other hand, there is the intense romantic relationship between Johnny and Gilda, who sings at the casino. The movie's complications arise because Gilda has married Ballin on the rebound from Johnny, becoming his property, and Johnny earns his livelihood by looking after everything that Ballin owns.

The movie takes its emotional energy from Johnny and Gilda's desire to punish one another for wrongs done in their earlier relationship. Gilda seems intent on driving Johnny mad with jealousy. She throws herself at other men in front of him. She refuses to do what he says unless he forces her to. But most of all, she wants to seduce every man in sight to prove to him he no longer means anything to her. She starts with individual patrons of the casino and ends up by putting on a floor show that causes men to stampede the stage.

Gilda plays on many themes that are familiar in temptress stories. The men are in control when they gamble with dice and cards but tread on treacherous ground when they try to extend their lucky streaks with women. After Ballin's marriage to Gilda, Johnny congratulates Gilda, rather than Ballin, on the advantageous match, and when Gilda calls from her bedroom, the infatuated Ballin, a successful businessman, comes running. Johnny makes a direct reference to the duplicity of women when he says Ballin's concealed weapon must be of the female persuasion because "it looks like one thing and right in front of your eyes it turns into another."

Ballin and Johnny have a strong, almost intimate relationship when it's just the two of them. It is Gilda who introduces chaos—surprise, surprise—when she enters their world. In her signature tune, "Put the Blame on Mame," natural disasters such as floods and earthquakes are attributed to Mame's power to disrupt the energy fields around her. Gilda, the child of nature, can make the earth move. Unlike the carefully planned machinations of other femmes fatales, chaos seems to flow naturally out of Gilda. Trying to win back Johnny is an emotional quest, and she doesn't give a damn what the fallout might be.

Gilda is clearly a temptress for a time when men were regaining their equilibrium, for in the end she begs her man for his affection. The last part of the movie plays out like a modern-day *Taming of the Shrew*. Johnny is intent on teaching Gilda a lesson. She rebels. Only when the two of them have pushed each other as far as they can do they allow themselves to call a truce and admit that they are made for each other. In true femme fatale style, Gilda does not triumph over Ballin and Johnny, but unlike the heroines of most films noirs, Gilda sees the error of her ways before it is too late. At the end of the movie Ballin is dead and Johnny and Gilda are looking forward to a

future together. There is no doubt that Johnny is going to be a strong shoulder for her to lean on as she assumes the traditional role of wife.

Throughout the movie, Rita Hayworth is the physical embodiment of the femme fatale. The classic femme fatale is tall with legs that seem to go on forever. She is feminine, but her femininity is to be found not in the depth of her cleavage but in her predatory demeanor and her catlike grace. It is to be experienced in the serpentine undulations of her walk and in her hypnotically slow, sensuous movements as she fondles objects around her. When Gilda sings "Put the Blame on Mame" softly to herself in the empty club, what man would not want to take the place of the guitar on her lap as she brushes her long, elegant fingers back and forth over the throbbing strings?

The femme fatale is often enigmatic, her motivations and emotions unclear, her past a story of broken dreams and broken promises. When she takes a drag on a cigarette in a long holder, she is enveloped in a cloud of smoke, and her face may be veiled or hidden under a large-brimmed hat. An aura of languor envelops her. When she speaks, her voice is low and husky. The interiors through which she moves are shadowed; the exterior landscapes are generic and oppressive. (Gilda herself is a child of the night, disappearing into the darkness with her men.) The audience's imagination fills in the gaps in the partially revealed picture— to chilling effect.

With her long legs and inner steel, there is a sense of the masculine about this temptress, but it is a masculinity that is shot through with a raw sensuality that is alien to men. The man in her sights responds to it, but he does not understand it. He is attracted and repelled at the same time. His conflicting emotions create the edge of tension on which the film noir rides.

The femme fatale seeks out a man who is willing to take risks, a man who is willing to bet all he has to pull off "the big one." If he hesitates, she pushes the action along. Her goal absorbs her totally, and she takes no notice of the everyday world that would limit her desires. She oversteps the bounds of common decency by a wide margin but doesn't care, and he is turned on by her audacity: her boldness thrills and chills. If the goddess of virtue is a lily and the vamp is an overripe red rose, the femme fatale is a Venus flytrap, waiting in the shadows to swallow up her chosen prey. And man is the intrepid explorer ready to chop her down.

THE TEMPTRESS is in a constant state of flux. Just as the vigorous vamp was ousted by the feisty blonde, so the sultry femme fatale has her counterpart. She is another blonde, but one that is softer around the edges than the blazing bombshell of the 1930s. The upswing of the temptress cycle of the 1950s produced the curvaceous and slightly wacky sex kitten.

Chapter 9

The Sex Kitten

As the war dust settled in the late forties, men were delighted when women packed up their bags of tools, stowed away their office organizers, and returned to the suburbs. And when they got there, they weren't leaving their marriages en masse or creating trouble as the image of the femme fatale had suggested they might. No, women in the fifties were smiling, producing happy families of rosy-cheeked children, and putting home-cooked evening meals on the table. Men's place in society was secure, after all.

As a result, the image of the temptress needed some adjustment once again. It was time for another one of those lovely blonde apparitions who stroke men in all the right places and don't ask too much in return. Right on cue, in walks Marilyn Monroe. Just as the bombshell counteracted the chills of the vamp, so the sex kitten was just the tonic men needed to recover from the femme fatale.

From the start, Marilyn Monroe had the same comfort with her body that Jean Harlow had exhibited with hers. In the famous scene from *The Seven-Year Itch,* she stands with her legs apart above a subway vent in New York, enjoying the upward rush of air from a passing train that sends her skirt flying around her shapely thighs. Once again, men are treated to a woman who is happy to reveal more flesh than is modest and who seems to take a positive delight in doing so. The fact that Monroe retained a wide-eyed innocence about the effect she had on men only added to her appeal. While filming one of her first movies, *Scudda Hoo! Scudda Hay!* in 1947, Monroe would turn up in the studio cafeteria wearing little fluffy pink sweaters with nothing underneath. Ben Lyon, who had brought her to Fox, once suggested to her that she dress better. When he had left, Monroe was heard to remark disingenuously, "I guess Ben doesn't like pink."

The femme fatale had brought with her motivation and schemes. A sex kitten like Monroe was far less complicated: you just had to look at her. It didn't take plot development for Monroe to project sex on the screen. When she made an entrance, sex wafted into the room with her. In *Love Happy*, a bomb of a film that was supposed to revive the flagging careers of the Marx brothers, the most memorable moment occurs when Monroe wiggles into the office of a private detective by the name of Grunion (played by Groucho Marx) and says, "Some men are following me." To which Marx responds, as she walks away swinging her amazing hips, "I can't imagine why."

Men were immediately attentive to Monroe's youth, vitality, and well-proportioned body. Even in modern times, sexual attraction is driven by the unconscious urge to transfer genes to the next generation, and in Monroe, men were presented with the perfect vessel for reproduction: a healthy young woman with generous hips. Even though fatherhood was the last thing on their minds when they laid eyes on her, they had no doubt they wanted her thanks to that primary evolutionary wiring.

Not only did Monroe look good, she also suggested that she would put out. While she was working on her image, Monroe studied the techniques of one Lili St. Cyr, a famous striptease artist of the 1950s. St. Cyr had perfected a show in which she suggested much while revealing little. Monroe was fascinated by St. Cyr's stage persona and from her learned to present moist lips and a slightly open mouth to the camera. The provocative combination of moistness and openness suggested that her lips just had been or soon would be employed providing pleasure to men. Thanks to St. Cyr, Monroe also developed her trademark smoldering, heavy-lidded, slightly sleepy gaze that seemed to announce, "I've just had mind-blowing sex with someone and the next time it could be with you." She was definitely available.

Also, there were Monroe's breasts. American men of the 1950s just couldn't get enough of the female chest. The torpedo-like breasts of wartime pinups had stiffened soldiers' fighting resolve as they decorated traveling kits and the nose cones of bomber aircraft. After all the men had been through, the thought of returning home and nuzzling their heads between generous, nourishing breasts was well-nigh irresistible. And Monroe had a cleavage that could rival the best of them.

And God Created Woman

I N 1956, a young Brigitte Bardot appeared in the movie *And God Created Woman* to show that woman had not lost her tangy, chaotic edge and that man—preferably a young, strong man—could still tame her.

Juliette (played by Bardot) is a wild orphan of seventeen who is going to be sent back to the orphanage because her foster mother cannot control

her. She flaunts her sexuality from the moment we see her naked feet protruding from behind a loaded clothesline. She is a potential mistress in the eyes of the elderly yacht owner, Mr. Carradine; a confirmed slut in the eyes of the ambitious businessman, Antoine; and a potential partner in the eyes of Antoine's naive younger brother, Michel.

Against all odds, Juliette agrees to marry Michel so that she will not be sent back to the orphanage, but later strains against the curtailment of her freedom in her mother-in-law's home. She wants to please her husband, but her as-yet-untamed nature is too strong. She visits the yacht owner who desires her, but Mr. Carradine fears that if he were to make her his mistress, he would become her slave. And then, after a tussle on the beach, Juliette and Antoine succumb to the heat of the moment, but their adulterous lovemaking merely confirms Antoine's view that she is too wanton to be an acceptable mate for any man.

Juliette's infidelity provokes a fight between the brothers and engenders in her a feeling of despair. She flees to the basement of a shady bar and abandons herself to the insistent beat of a traveling calypso band. Neither Mr. Carradine nor Antoine wants to invest in her further, but Michel is willing to try to reel her in. The audience is left with the strong suspicion that he will succeed—and that his efforts will be richly rewarded. The barefoot child of nature will surely make a satisfying wife once her vitality has been appropriately channeled.

Monroe had one final sexual ace up her nonexistent sleeve. She combined a knowing sexuality with the innocence and vulnerability of a little girl. She breathed her words in a small, little-girl voice guaranteed to bring out the big protector in whatever man was by her side. As a woman she promised sex and as a child she promised to be delightfully open to suggestion and eager to please. Like the femme fatale who embodied the tension between feminine charm and masculine aggression, Monroe's sex kitten was an electric juxtaposition of womanly experience and childish innocence rolled into one delightfully wiggling package.

In Monroe's early films, her walk-on parts were brief and she could barely act, but her lack of polish mattered not a whit. She had that look, that walk, and that breathy little-girl voice, all of which were guaranteed to make men melt. Men who fantasized about inviting a femme fatale into their lives were asking for many sleepless nights, but men who fantasized about the sex kitten had no such problems. Monroe was a squeezable feminine treat who seemed open to enjoying sex. Period. And, most delightful of all, the men she fell for in her movies were not typical Hollywood hunks. She had a heart of gold and would go where she was needed to perk men up. Now this kind of woman was good to have around.

In the 1950s, movies had to compete with the increasingly popular medium of television. The advantage movie producers had was the ability to show more sex on the big screen than was considered proper in people's homes, and they knew it. The movie moguls ordered Monroe sewn into gowns and swimsuits that squeezed every drop of sexuality from her arresting figure. At the same time, she was presented as not overly educated, so she wouldn't show up any man. In *The Seven-Year Itch*, her lack of "book *facing page:* The real stars of Howard Hughes's 1943 movie *The Outlaw* were Jane Russell's breasts. Hughes spent weeks designing a bra that would show them off to their best advantage. A Maryland judge who banned the film complained that Russell's breasts hung over the picture "like a thunderstorm spread over a landscape."

learning" is all part of her charm. She doesn't recognize Rachmaninov, but she knows it must be classical music because it has no vocals. She sums up her philosophy in *Gentlemen Prefer Blondes:* "I can be smart when it's important, but most men don't like it." "Look good and we'll love you," the men say. "Okay," she says. "Get an eyeful of this."

Monroe is irresistible to men because she promises to have no existence beyond pleasuring them. The subtext is that she enjoys sex and is happy to dispense it whenever men want. They do not need to feel guilty about wanting her, because she thinks it entirely natural that they do. It's what she's there for. She will not interfere in how they run the world because she neither understands nor cares. All she needs is to be looked after. And on top of it all, she has a zest for life and experience that is guaranteed to put the flash back into the most jaded of men, like a kind of psychological Viagra. No wonder the men lined up to see her movies, and no wonder her image still decorates the walls of cafés and diners around the world.

THE SWING FROM femme fatale to sex kitten marked another temptress cycle successfully survived by the men of this world. The femme fatale faded out as the perky blonde burst through the door just looking for men who wanted to enjoy her body. The machinations, the plots, the endless agonies of deceit unraveled as quickly as men hoped those straining light-pink sweaters would if they tugged on the right piece of yarn. By the 1950s, according to the gods in Hollywood, women had little more than snagging a husband on their minds and were once again objects for men's sexual enjoyment. The sun had come up again and all was right with the world.

Chapter 10

The Matron and the Nymphet

The sixties were a relatively relaxed interlude in the battle between the sexes. With the advent of the birth-control pill, sex for pleasure—and for everyone—suddenly seemed like a possibility. It was a time to play with the image of the temptress to see how many different aspects she could embrace. And, as the main focus of the decade was youth against age, it is hardly surprising that two potent temptresses from this era should explore the generation gap. On screen, the unforgettable society matron Mrs. Robinson seduces an innocent young college graduate, while in Vladimir Nabokov's late fifties novel *Lolita*, a preteen temptress works her magic on a middle-aged professor of literature whose sexual imagination has never worked itself free of his first childhood love.

Mrs. Robinson

Although older women do sometimes pair off with younger men, this kind of coupling is the exception rather than the norm. Darwinian theorists explain that what a woman looks for in a mate is a powerful male with resources to invest in offspring, because such a protector will give her children a better chance of survival. It usually takes time for men to acquire power and wealth, and so women tend to choose partners older than they are. A man, however, is looking for health and vitality, signs that a woman will be able to conceive and will survive childbirth, thus maximizing his chances of passing on his genetic material. Since these attributes are usually found in young women, men tend to choose mates younger than they are.

In theory, women who choose younger men as mates may do so because they have so many resources of their own that they don't care whether the men are good providers or not. In another of those subtle gender shifts that happen often in temptress relationships, the older woman who goes for the younger man may be looking for the health and vitality men usually seek in women—not for reproduction, but to relive physical sensations that are rapidly becoming mere memories. The older woman wants the adrenaline edge of unexpected sex, and she likes the idea of being in the driver's seat. Luckily, that is where the kind of young man who falls for an older woman's charms wants her to be.

From the start of the 1967 classic *The Graduate*, Mrs. Robinson is the aggressor. At the end of her friends' party in honor of their son Ben's graduation from college, she tracks Ben down in his bedroom, lights up a provocative cigarette in front of the clean-living college athlete, and asks him for a ride home. Ben is shy, but his body looks promising and he is definitely meek enough to be commanded. When he tells her she can drive herself home in his car, she pleads ignorance of the workings of a stick shift.

When they arrive at her house the seduction continues. Will he come in?

No? But she's afraid to be alone and courtesy dictates a nightcap. The noisy clink of the ice cubes deposited in Ben's glass warns that Mrs. Robinson is not a woman who will take no for an answer. Ben tries to assert himself. Then he panics. Mrs. Robinson remains cool while Ben's emotions skitter all over the map. Finally he says—with a note of pride, as though he's figured out the answer to an especially pesky math problem—"Mrs. Robinson, you're trying to seduce me." Mrs. Robinson swears that the idea, intriguing as it is, has never occurred to her.

Now Ben has got to make it up to her in some way, and that is how she gets him upstairs to admire a portrait of her daughter, Elaine. As Mrs. Robinson begins to take off her jewelry, Ben concentrates hard on keeping up the charade that she is not seducing him, but when she asks for his help undressing, he can't bring himself to touch her zipper. As Ben tries to escape down the stairs, Mrs. Robinson accuses him of not wanting to render her a simple service. Ben's nerves are now so taut that he's ready to bolt. Mrs. Robinson turns the key in the lock. Whatever happens next, it is not of Ben's doing. He will have been forced into it against his will. Well, passively against his will. Well, put it this way: he never asked her to take off her clothes.

Men are usually expected to make the first move, and Ben seems perplexed yet relieved to have bypassed that nerve-racking step. It is better this way. Much better. She is naked and he is fully clothed. She becomes an object for him to admire. He averts his gaze and looks, averts his gaze and looks. Women his mother's age are not supposed to act this way and are definitely not supposed to look this good. Mrs. Robinson knows that Ben will not be able to get the sight of her bare breasts out of his mind. The seed has been sown. All she has to do is wait.

When we next see Ben, he is wearing scuba-diving gear and preparing to enter the family pool while his parents and friends watch. From underwater, his familiar world appears far away and indistinct and he tries to acclimatize himself to his unfamiliar element. Once he does, he realizes he likes the new lens through which he is filtering his world. A few days later, shaking uncontrollably, he calls Mrs. Robinson to arrange a meeting at the Taft Hotel.

At the hotel, it is obvious Ben is making progress. He's drinking and smoking. He's still not assertive enough to get the waiter's attention when Mrs. Robinson wants a drink, however, so she shows him how it's done. She is amused by his maladroit behavior, by his failure to realize that he's invited her up to his room but forgotten to give her the room number. She is the indulgent mother watching as he takes his first steps, the indulgent teacher who wants her student to succeed.

Once they are in the room, she takes the lead. When he turns off the lights, she turns them on again. When he does not know what to do next, she has a suggestion. When he makes a false start, she sets the process back on track. He doesn't need to worry about his fumbling because this is what charms her about him. His fear of inadequacy is not a deterrent but an aphrodisiac. She already has a successful man of the world, and her marriage has stifled her zest for life. Ben's youth and innocence give her the chance to regain—if only fleetingly—what she has lost. And he is thrilled and relieved that he has something she wants.

facing page: Ben may have graduated from college, but he is not yet ready, in Mrs. Robinson's opinion, for the big wide world. She sets about filling in the gaps in his education.

Mrs. Robinson's attraction to masculine ineptitude in the bedroom feeds a fantasy that is soothing to many men. In a world where men are supposed to be innately gifted studs, a woman who gives clear directions and feedback on what works and what does not is a huge relief. No more guessing games. No more fear of reprimand. When Ben doubts his ability to follow through, Mrs. Robinson taunts him about being inadequate and then makes as if to leave; the fear of losing her gives him the shot of adrenaline he requires, and he rises to the challenge.

Although the sixties were liberal, people were still on the fence when it came to intergenerational sex. As a result, the temptress, true to type, turns out to be a selfish woman who has only her own pleasure in mind. The delight Mrs. Robinson has to offer cannot sustain Ben for long, and his relationship with the older woman turns out to be a detour from his main task: finding a loyal, loving, younger woman with whom he can settle down.

By the end of the movie, what Ben desires above all else is not the sexy, experienced Mrs. Robinson but her chaste daughter, Elaine. Just as Greek sailors saw Sirens revealed in their true forms when they stopped singing, so Ben sees the ugly side of Mrs. Robinson when he defies her orders not to date Elaine. Underneath her seductive exterior, Mrs. Robinson is an old hag with the claws of a Harpy and the snakelike locks of a Gorgon. Ben must escape from her clutches before it is too late.

Had it been a more repressive decade, Mrs. Robinson would likely have destroyed Ben. Luckily for Ben, however, the sixties were devoted to chilling out, and Mrs. Robinson's power dissolves in the face of youth and true love. The young, virtuous woman prevails over the wily temptress, and Elaine is even willing to forgive Ben for sleeping with her mother. Once Ben has received his sexual education from a woman of experience, he's eager to resume his dominant position with a woman who has none. Ben really can have his cake and eat it, too.

There is a hint, however, that audiences at the time might have been ready to embrace real change. In the final shot, Ben and Elaine are not sitting together but apart, and Ben appears to be thinking not of their shared future but of his immediate past. The audience is left to wonder if Ben has made the right choice. Is Elaine really the better prize, or should he have kicked convention and accepted the inconceivable—that Mrs. Robinson might have been the woman for him, after all?

Lolita

Ben, it is clear, has choices. Humbert Humbert, who stalks Lolita in the novel of the same name, is not so lucky. He too gets to live his fantasies, but there is no escape at the end of his tunnel. This is because he has chosen territory far more dangerous than Ben did: sexual desire for a child.

Whereas Mrs. Robinson carefully orchestrated every step of her seduction of Ben, Lolita seduces merely through existing. Humbert has been primed by past experience and personal predilection to react to her on sight; the moment he sees twelve-year-old Lolita in his landlady's garden, he knows he must have her, even if he must suppress his disgust and marry his landlady first to achieve his goal.

At the outset Lolita is completely innocent of guile, but her power over Humbert is no less complete. Everything about her is to him a Siren's call: "Why does the way she walks . . . excite me so abominably?" he asks himself. "A faint suggestion of turned in toes. A kind of wiggly looseness below

the knee prolonged to the end of each footfall." These are not characteristics likely to arouse any male but one supremely attuned to the nuances of nonchalant youth before the onset of sexual awareness. Even her vulgarity, her "slangy speech," so at odds with Humbert's European sensitivities, turns him on. She is seen utterly, completely, through his own personal viewfinder. Not surprisingly, he finds her irresistible.

Lolita accepts that she is desirable, even though she has no comprehension of exactly how this man desires her. Gradually, seeing herself relentlessly reflected in his gaze, she learns to manipulate his passions. It takes her much longer to figure out how to escape them, and by the time she does, her childhood has been consumed by the intensity of Humbert's desire for her and her desire to be free.

The moment Humbert sets eyes on Lolita, he is reminded of his first love, Annabel, now lost, who haunts his memory. Humbert's past experiences have programmed him for arousal the moment Lolita appears in his life. She is a temptress—but only because he makes her one. Humbert plants the seed of seduction in Lolita. She is, he assures the reader, a nymphet, the kind of seductive child that he is uniquely equipped to recognize: "You have to be an artist and a madman . . . in order to discern at once, by ineffable signs—

the slightly feline outline of a cheekbone, the slenderness of a downy limb, and other indices which despair and shame and tears of tenderness forbid me to tabulate—the little deadly demon among the wholesome children." But in the same breath, he acknowledges her innocence: "*She* stands unrecognized by them and unconscious herself of her fantastic power," and his guilt: "Oh, how you have to cringe and hide!"

Humbert marries Lolita's mother to be close to the child, and when the mother is killed in an accident, he contrives a road trip with the daughter that starts the way he fervently hoped it would. After he has agonized over how to rent a single room for the two of them and just how to approach her and whether he could sedate her in order to ravish her while she is sleeping, he is taken completely unawares when she is the one to propose that she demonstrate her sexual prowess on him. They become lovers.

The couple settles down briefly together as father and daughter in a college town, where Humbert has an academic position and where Lolita is enrolled in a girls' school. Lolita, more aware of her power over Humbert than ever, begins to demand money for sexual favors. Humbert finds that his world is unraveling as the object of his lust turns out to have a distressingly independent will of her own. There are also signs that the gash Humbert has opened in Lolita's psyche is widening, allowing in more sexual predators than the one who longs to rule alone.

When Lolita chafes at the relationship, Humbert packs her into their car, hoping to outrun the inevitable. Lolita is surprisingly compliant. Although Humbert knows that his mad rush across the country with his darling cannot last, he cannot help himself. He still tells himself that she has "the body of some immortal daemon disguised as a female child," and that therefore the physical yearnings in every fiber of his being must emanate from her. This tale might have been convincing in the era of Eve or Pandora, but the modern, aching Humbert knows that despite his efforts to view Lolita as a timeless, heartless spirit, the depravity that has drawn him to her lies deep within his own soul. Her flight into the arms of Quilty, a pedophile even more heartless than Humbert, is one for which he has laid the groundwork.

Even when Lolita escapes into the arms of the lascivious Quilty and then into the arms of a poor but honest husband, she retains her hold on Humbert's imagination. He can never shake his love for the nymphet. He will come when she calls, offering her assistance, and asks for nothing in return. But he has already taken so much from her. The accidental seductress gains some measure of recompense when Humbert shoots Quilty and serves time for his crime, but for Lolita, her childhood can never be regained. For Humbert, the reality of Lolita spills out like an ugly ink blot over his fantasy of the lost Annabel. His longing to recapture the love of his youth would have been better left to the world of dreams.

THE SIXTIES came right after the invention of the birth control pill and right before the emergence of the feminist movement. There were unprecedented opportunities for sexual experimentation and little sense yet that women were poised to make a grab for power. Men seized the chance to play with the temptress image, creating her as young or old to see which incarnation would be most delightful and to find where the limits of acceptable seductive fantasies might fall. It would not be long, however, before the gains made by women in the following decades caused men's blood pressure to rise once again, and temptresses became more demanding.

James Bond's Women

. . . .

ONE FANTASY image born in the sixties that has endured into the twenty-first century—albeit with some modifications to update her image—is the gorgeous deadly spy who stalks the fearless British agent 007, James Bond. Over the years, this lovely lady has borrowed the lingerie of the sex kitten, stepped into the high heels of the enigmatic femme fatale, and assumed the sexual independence of the sixties playmate. The vamp and two world wars long forgotten, she is no match for the slick-talking, handsome male spy equipped with the very latest technology that Q has to offer. True to the conservative element in the pre-feminist era that gave rise to her, she is a woman who exists to be overcome.

In movie after movie, Bond can indulge in sexual dalliance with the most beautiful women his world has to offer, confident that his advances will be welcomed, his desires will be sated, and his satisfaction will not dull his finely tuned sense of impending danger. Even with the most deadly of his female foes, there is usually some spark of connection—of emotions shared or of mutual physical pleasure—that shows that deep in the fiber of their being, they cannot resist his masculinity.

This temptress fantasy has proven so satisfying that Bond continues to be paired up with beautiful women intent on his destruction. In a nod to advances made by women, the beautiful spies have become more cunning, more powerful, and more muscular, but Bond still happily beds them and then outwits them every time. Here at last is a modern Odysseus who does not need to be lashed to the mast when the Sirens sing. Ears unwaxed and hands (most often) free, he sails confidently into the seas of danger, experiences bliss, and escapes unharmed.

Chapter 11

The Ultimate Bitch

After the burst of flower power and free love in the sixties, feminists made a concerted effort to improve the lot of women. By 1963, U.S. federal law required equal compensation for men and women in federal jobs, and by 1964 the Civil Rights Act prohibited job discrimination on the basis of sex. In 1974 the first woman governor was elected and in 1981, the first female Supreme Court justice was appointed. In 1992, more women in the United States ran for, and were elected to, political office than in any other year in the nation's history. Elsewhere in the world, the United Nations declared 1975 to 1985 a Decade for Women. Ten years later, in 1995, the UN hosted a human rights conference in Beijing, China, focused on women's issues. As the twentieth century clicked over into the twenty-first, advances continued as women began to crack glass ceilings and achieve educations equal to or surpassing those of men.

Against this backdrop of women's progress, spikes of male anxiety occasionally break through. The peaks of fear often take the form of ultra-conservative or religious movements that call for the return of the wife to her traditional place: in the home and firmly behind her man. The Promise

Keepers, for example, a male-only religious movement started in 1990, exhort men to reclaim their places at the heads of their households. The iceberg tips of anxiety demonstrated by such movements are also reflected in the appearance, from the seventies to the end of the twentieth century, of movies that portray a chilling new type of temptress, the ultimate bitch: a woman who is intelligent, well educated, and successful—yet morally and sexually out of control.

In *Basic Instinct*, Sharon Stone plays a ruthless temptress called Catherine Tramell. The movie opens at the moment of orgasm. Just when the victim is at his most vulnerable, he is stabbed to death with an ice pick by the naked woman who has brought him to his climax. The woman is, not surprisingly, on top. This has been men's worst nightmare all along: sex with a beautiful but dangerous woman as the ultimate self-destructive act. The scene is also a beautiful illustration of the nineteenth-century theory of seminal fluids, which postulates that a man's store of semen is finite and that depleted stocks weaken men. As the murder victim's semen is being pumped out of him, so is his blood. Just as the Victorians had suspected, each ejaculation brings a man that much closer to death.

As in the 1940s film noir, the main male character in *Basic Instinct* is a man who has sworn to uphold law and order. Michael Douglas plays Nick Curran, a San Francisco detective who is investigating the ice-pick murder. In *Double Indemnity*, Neff was an insurance salesman who was good at what he did but who had not advanced far in his job. In *Basic Instinct*, Nick is more obviously flawed. He is a reformed alcoholic and drug addict, and he has been in trouble on the job for his overactive trigger finger. Catherine has researched a possible departmental cover-up in the case of a couple of tourists shot to death by Nick, and there are seething tensions running through the male-buddy department in which he operates. Operating at the margins of the ordered male world, Catherine, in classic temptress fashion, will exploit Nick's weaknesses and the departmental tensions to her own ends.

In *Basic Instinct*, the impact of the woman's physical presence is the first dropped stitch in a sequence of events that threaten to unravel the man's world. Catherine is tall, cool, and blonde. She is acutely aware of—and amused by—the effect her appearance has on men. She parades her sexuality before the police officers investigating the murder and frankly tells them how much she enjoyed sex with the victim. On two separate occasions Nick watches from the shadows as she peels off her clothes to stand naked in front of the plate-glass windows of her house. In the famous interrogation scene near the beginning of the movie, she slowly and deliberately uncrosses and then re-crosses her legs to reveal to the law-enforcement officers a stunning lack of underwear under her short, tight skirt, all the while smiling at their discomfiture.

Catherine makes it clear that for her sex is an act of physical gratification rather than emotional connection. This attitude runs counter to everything men are told about women. It is how men are supposed to view sex; it is not how sensitive, caring females are supposed to feel. Catherine is ultra-feminine in her sex appeal and ultra-masculine in her assessment of the sex act itself. The tension that arises in Nick as he tries to reconcile these opposites excites him.

Like a femme fatale, Catherine engages both Nick's sex drive and his competitive instincts. She makes him want her when she flaunts her body and then challenges him to take her when she engages his mind. Nick rises to the bait. His task, as he sees it, is to turn a woman who toys with men for her own personal pleasure into a contented contributor to a traditional male-female partnership. He is confident he can do this. What he doesn't know is that his confidence is all part of her master plan.

Catherine knows how important it is to get Nick imagining himself as her lover. In the interrogation room she singles him out for attention and kick-starts his imagination by suggesting there are many ways to make love to her: "I don't make any rules, Nick," she says. "I go with the flow."

When Nick takes the bait and suggests that she likes it when men use their hands, Catherine corrects him. She liked it, she says, when the murder victim used his hands. Nick now knows that when he makes love to her, he will be special, the only one who will be able to give her pleasure quite the way he does. To make sure the hook takes hold, Catherine then gets Nick imagining specific scenarios with her. "Have you ever fucked on cocaine, Nick?" she asks. After the provocative leg cross gives him a moment to think about this possibility, she finishes the thought: "It's nice."

Catherine wants Nick to know she is a catch worth having. She gives the detectives to understand that she can have sex whenever and wherever she wants it. When asked if she was with someone the night of the murder, she replies that she was alone—but only because she wasn't in the mood that night. She's a woman who clearly has choices. The ease with which she finds sexual partners contrasts with the dismal sex lives of Nick and his partner, Gus, who report that they have to resort to masturbation (Nick) or blue-haired old ladies (Gus) if they want to get their rocks off. The two detectives have to work hard for their dates, but both men and women are drawn to Catherine like moths to a flame.

This late-twentieth-century temptress is terrifyingly intelligent and she has the education to prove it. She graduated magna cum laude from Berkeley with two degrees—one in psychology and one in literature. She has the knowledge and the desire to mess not just with men's bodies but with their minds. Nick first believes Catherine to be guilty of murder and then, after sleeping with her, changes his mind. To his down-to-earth partner, Gus, there is no mystery to his change of heart: "She's got that magna cum laude pussy on her that done fried up your brain." Nick is convinced Gus is wrong.

Catherine considers herself above the petty rules men make to govern their lives. She ignores them completely (as when she lights up in a non-smoking zone at the police station while being interrogated), sidesteps them (as when she outwits the lie-detector machine), or uses her knowledge of them to push events the way she wants them to go (as when she makes the detectives believe another woman is responsible for Gus's eventual murder).

In control at every turn, she is a thrill-seeker who pushes experiences to the limit to increase her high. She drives like a maniac, leading Nick on a wild chase on the twisting mountain roads of California. Nick's nerves eventually give out when he narrowly misses a head-on collision with a truck, and he decides to risk losing her rather than his life. But the car chase is just the warm-up to a more intimate thrill. When Nick and Catherine first make love, she ties him to the bed frame in exactly the same way that the murder victim was tied. It is a game of chicken. Will he allow her to do this to him, even though he suspects her of murder? She knows exactly what is going on in his mind and knows that his fear will intensify his orgasm. It does. To the ecstatic Nick, it is "the fuck of the century." After their lovemaking, when no ice pick is forthcoming, Nick believes he has stared down the enemy and survived.

At the end of the movie, Catherine turns up at Nick's apartment after Gus's murder to make sure that Nick does not suspect her of the crime. She wins Nick over with a finely nuanced performance of despair and neediness, knowing full well that this is the moment he has been waiting for. Assured of her vulnerability and need for him, he makes love to her to show her that he can ease her pain.

When Catherine asks Nick what they will do now, she is ready to reach for the ice pick if he shows any sign of realizing how she has manipulated him. His response makes it clear that there is not a shred of suspicion on his part. He believes that he has reached the soft core at the center of her being and that she is ready to set aside her vendetta against the world and become his contented helpmeet. As the camera lingers over the ice pick hidden under the bed, we, the audience, are not so sure.

In *Basic Instinct*, a film noir for the nineties, the man is more flawed and the woman more independent than in previous stories of this type. She doesn't need him for money or power; she has plenty of that on her own. The battle between the sexes played out in the seventies and eighties has left men deeply distrustful of women's ultimate goals. Women have achieved equality in education (Catherine's magna cum laude degree), in their careers (Catherine's job as a successful writer), and in social position (Catherine's immense wealth). And yet men are left with the feeling that women want more. What more could they possibly want?

The psychopathic character of Catherine Tramell, with her intricately laid plans of destruction, is an attempt to answer this question. Here is a woman who considers herself superior to men, and look what happens. She is not content to sit at home and write her books. She has to go out and create

chaos in the lives of those around her. She is the ultimate bitch. She succeeds because when Nick has to make a choice between the solid woman who will stand by his side and the dangerous woman who will betray him, the hero cannot resist pursuing the risky character. Both women are beautiful and sexy, but only one smells of danger, and winning her will mean so much more to a man who needs to prove himself.

The ultimate bitch seeks out a man who has buttons she can push. She accurately predicts his reactions until it seems that he is a marionette and she is pulling his strings. Gus, who can see her more clearly, warns Nick that he has "damn tweetie birds in his head" if he thinks the two of them will live happily ever after. But Nick will not listen. He is interested enough in her to pursue her and arrogant enough to believe that she will fall for him. He is the perfect target for her attentions.

THIS CAUTIONARY TALE for the nineties reflects men's fear of women who have made many gains in status. Because these women still want more, they are not to be trusted. The margin of male supremacy has dwindled significantly. Now, more than ever, it is important to make sure that the two sides never become truly equal. The clever, successful, beautiful woman really is too good to be true, men warn. Those who think they have figured out her treachery gesticulate wildly from behind soundproof glass, hoping the men on the other side will get their message before it is too late.

Fatal Attractions

. . . .

As FEMINISTS made inroads into areas of male privilege in the latter half of the twentieth century, the pendulum swung between male anxiety and accommodation. Three movies chart the progress of the female psychopath. This type appeared, then faded, as men accommodated themselves to each successive female advance.

In *Play Misty for Me* (1971) and *Fatal Attraction* (1987), beneath the woman's unassumingly normal exterior lies a creature who is, literally, insane. The radio deejay played by Clint Eastwood in *Play Misty for Me* opens his door to a beautiful woman who seems to want nothing more than a one-night stand. When he spurns her advances, she turns to murder. In *Fatal Attraction*, when Michael Douglas's character agrees to a night of no-holds-barred sex believing there will be no strings attached, he has entered the spider's web. Glenn Close's character is relentless and violent in her pursuit of the man she wants all to herself. In both movies, with the support of his steadfast, loving partner, the man eventually triumphs over the evil temptress. Some women may be breaking the rules, these movies suggest, but thanks to those who remain true, the men are not beaten—yet.

By the time of *The Last Seduction* (1994), matters have taken a more sinister turn as men can see the gap between men's and women's privileges in the real world fading fast. In this movie, it is not the man that the woman wants, but the avenues to power that he can open up for her. Here, there is no redemption for men; the fatal woman is too evil, too calculating, too fiendishly clever to be stopped. Linda Fiorentino's character, like Catherine Tramell, is a warning for the late-twentieth-century male. Once women have enough power to be independent of men, they may seduce men just to get what they want and then do away with them altogether.

Chapter 12

Women on Top

Traditionally, men have been the tellers of temptress tales. They have constructed stories that reflect their fantasies and their fears. They have imagined women with the power to destroy them, women over whom they triumph, and women they search for and can never quite find. Gradually, women have found their own voices and their own ways to play back their sexuality to men. Many of these take-charge women have been performers who have used the stage to parade the seduction fantasies in which they star. An early proponent of female autonomy in the story-telling department was Mae West, who spent the teen years and the Roaring Twenties strutting her stuff on stages across America before outraging Hollywood censors with her woman-on-top routine in the 1930s.

Mae West

The indomitable Mae West started her stage career at the age of thirteen. She spent the next twenty-five years as a burlesque and vaudeville performer before making her assault on Hollywood in the summer of 1932 at an almost overripe thirty-eight. By the time she became a movie star, she had perfected a picture of voluptuous femininity accented with form-fitting gowns, oversized jewels, and exotic feathers. One reviewer of her play *Sex* wrote of her "emanating from her body the radiance of rhinestones and the fragrance of many bottles of insistent perfumes." When she got to Hollywood, she told the women who fitted her gowns, "I like 'em tight, girls." From her teens to well into her eighties, she specialized in characters who celebrated sexuality as a pleasure to be indulged—with the woman making all the choices.

Before West arrived in Tinseltown, she was primarily famous for having written and starred in *Sex*, which landed her in jail for ten days for indecency on the strength of a police officer's testimony that during her performance, he "saw something in her middle that moved from east to west." Undaunted, West told reporters her nine days in jail (she got one day off for good behavior) gave her a much-needed vacation and the opportunity to gather firsthand material for future plays about the seamier side of life. Her characters were invariably women who ignored prevailing moral standards and granted ample favors to men, yet who adhered to their own firmly held convictions about decency and fair play. In West's world, men were always there for the taking and willingly succumbed to her charms.

West never lost faith in the impact of her physical presence. One of her earliest stage performances was a dance with artfully arranged fans concealing her nakedness. Then she progressed to the shimmy, an exhibition piece she picked up at the black clubs. During her performance at the Majestic Theater in Chicago in 1917, she shook on stage with such gusto that the sequins flew off her gown. But West didn't need erotic movement to exude sex. She stole the show at the Schubert Theater on Broadway the next year merely by walking on stage.

Neither did she need explicit vocabulary. At her trial for *Sex,* the prosecutor could not find a single lewd line in the play but contended: "Miss West's personality, looks, walk, mannerisms, and gestures made the lines and situations suggestive." After seeing her play *Diamond Lil,* an appreciative Leonard Hall of New York's *Evening Telegram* wrote that the mere fact of West's presence was to men "what a hot fire is to a shivering wienerwurst." By the time she reached Hollywood, she had perfected a languorous, hand-on-hip slouch that complemented the husky delivery of her lines.

West often said that her art depended on rhythm, timing, and inflection, especially in the early thirties when she went head-to-head with Hollywood censors, who erased her most blatantly sexual lines, leaving West to rely heavily on the art of suggestion to get a rise out of her audience. West perfected pregnant pauses filled with expectation, and when words did come out of her mouth they positively dripped sex. Actor Anthony Quinn wrote in his autobiography, *The Original Sin,* that when he auditioned for a part in a proposed stage show in 1940, she asked him, "What do you do?" To Quinn, the four simple words encompassed at least "four different levels" of meaning. West never lost her ability to charge the most innocent of statements with sexual invitation. *Variety* magazine wrote that she "couldn't sing a lullaby without making it sexy," and toward the end of her career, she was reputed to have a voice that rasped with innuendo even when it was "offering you tea and toast."

When West arrived in Hollywood in 1932, she curled celluloid with her smoldering presence. She dyed her hair the prevailing Hollywood color of startling blonde and set to work. A critic described a typical entrance: "There was a terrific explosion. A bomb had gone off in a cream-puff factory. . . .

facing page: Mae West reveled in excess—the more sparkles the better. She studded her costumes and her repartee with glittering gems to lure and to amaze.

Blonde, buxom, rowdy Mae—slithering across the screen in a spangled, sausage-skin gown."

West disdained the willowy contours of standard Hollywood beauties, and although she had a cleavage that Anthony Quinn described as "dizzying," she was most proud of her hips. She did try dieting once, getting her weight down to 103 pounds, but she hated the overall effect and quickly replenished her curves. Barely five feet tall, she favored high heels to make her legs look longer and long, low-cut, jewel-encrusted gowns that accentuated every undulation of her flesh. One critic described her silhouette as "upholstered egg cup," but this, to West, was what being a woman was all about. In 1919, *Variety* had called her gown "very tasteful"—the first and last time that these words were used to describe West, who preferred to go overboard, all the time.

West was a firm believer in sex for fun. "I'm the girl who lost her reputation and never missed it," she once proclaimed. She had no problem with women instigating sex, and she believed that "a man himself doesn't know what he's capable of, until he gets the inspiration . . . from the woman he needs." Of her own reactions to the opposite sex, she wrote: "When I am attracted to a man, I am like an Amazon in battle; I hit out in all directions." She complained bitterly about the restrictions put on her by a male-dominated movie industry that did not share her open-minded views. "In the films, they wouldn't let me sit on a man's lap. And I've been on more laps than a napkin," she railed.

West spent most of her career writing, directing, and acting her own material, convinced that only she knew how best to present the West persona to the public. This—and her habit of obliterating others who vied for a piece of

her spotlight—occasionally made her a trial to work with. Director Lowell
Sherman apologized to scriptwriter John Bright, whose material was
constantly being changed: "Sorry, baby, but I have to handle the bitch-
goddess on the set."

As a woman who set her own rules, West expected performance from her
acting partners. She looked them over for physique and stage presence to see
if they would make acceptable backgrounds to highlight her talents. She also
expected a certain level of enthusiasm on a personal level. "It's not the men
in your life, but the life in your men that counts," her character Tira once
avowed. West's personal sexual appetite was reportedly voracious, and she
considered frequent sex a prerequisite for good health. When she posed for
the cover of *Vanity Fair* as the Statue of Liberty, critic George Jean Nathan
commented: "She looks more like the Statue of Libido." West, however, had

no problem with men openly enjoying the way she looked. When members of Britain's Royal Air Force called the lifejackets they wore "Mae Wests," she proudly announced that the moniker was "a tribute to my sex appeal in practical form."

Despite her excesses, the ever-pragmatic West acknowledged that there was still a gap between life and art. When she had the starring role in her play *Catherine Was Great*, she said: "Catherine was a great empress. She also had three hundred lovers. I did the best I could in a couple of hours." She seems to have had no difficulty keeping a stream of lovers going throughout her lifetime and even as she aged remained acutely interested in sex. At a party she attended for male entertainers in the 1960s, when she was in her seventies, she remarked: "My favorite audience, wall to wall men."

Throughout her career, on stage and off, West drew musclemen around her as members of a supporting and adoring cast. Whereas most women coyly accepted men's ogling, West actively and unabashedly ogled back. As her character Tira says when approaching a hunky acrobat admirer in *I'm No Angel*, "I'm not gonna to hurt him; I only want to feel his muscles." The character was to be billed as "the only girl who has satisfied more patrons than Chesterfields"—until Hollywood censors objected to the allusion and had the line cut.

West had a scant two years to exploit her new medium before censors began to shut her down, excising the lewd innuendoes and suggestive situations that were integral to her high-charged version of a woman of suspect sexual morality but with a heart of gold. Eventually, even the feisty West could not withstand the tide of decency that was to sweep away the brassy bad girl who was happy to lavishly share her charms and replace her with the dark, manipulative beauty who plotted men's demise from the shadowy rain-drenched street corners of film noir.

Women were not supposed to be as frank about their sexuality as West was about hers, but West saw nothing wrong with making it clear that women enjoy sex as much as men do and like to be satisfied. Her antidote to a society that had spent decades hiding women away in drawing rooms was to take the stage as boldly as any man. In her stories, the leading lady never allows her men to push her around, preferring to have them at her beck and call. She values her independence and commits herself to matrimony only "as a last resort." She has a steady stream of ardent admirers lining up for the privilege of spending a few hours in her company, her arms, her bed. She is supremely confident in her power to fascinate: "Once I get 'em, they're branded," says Lady Lou in *She Done Him Wrong*. And she would never sell herself short: "Anything different costs more, but it's worth it," Tira assures a would-be lover. When another tells her that he will never forget her, she doesn't doubt it: "No one ever does," she replies.

Although West takes a page from the traditional-male book when she acts aggressively with her lovers, she is also capable of traditionally female acts of seduction—although, as with everything West did, taken to extremes. Cary Grant, her co-star in a number of movies, once avowed: "I never worked with anyone who has as much 'she' as Mae West." And, in a radio script written for her in 1937, writer Arch Oboler has West's Eve seducing not only Adam in the Garden of Eden but also the serpent.

West also believed in giving credit where credit was due. As much as she enjoyed dispensing sexual favors, she recognized that it was the seemingly bottomless wellspring of desire within men that allowed her to. She was happy to provide the circumstance and let nature run its course. When a character in *I'm No Angel* says, "I don't see how any man could help loving you," she replies, "I don't give them any help. They do it themselves." Supremely confident of her sexual charms, she is convinced that any man would be grateful to spend time with her. When her driver in *She Done Him Wrong* mentions that her boudoir looks like Heaven, she doesn't hesitate: "That's why you've got to climb stairs to get there."

In all her performances, West had enormous fun. Her enjoyment of sexual dalliance and her belief in herself as irresistible turned her into what director Lowell Sherman called "America's wet dream." But these qualities also gave rise to outrage and unease and, eventually, ridicule—when she persisted in playing a well-preserved siren at the grand old age of eighty-five. Many men found West unbearably forward and her methods crude. It was acceptable, even expected, that men would lust after women; in the 1930s, however, they did not expect the compliment to be returned.

Men became increasingly uncomfortable with the way that West was invading their turf, and as the 1940s approached and the femme fatale was in the making, people began to snigger that she wasn't really a woman at all. She became at best "the greatest female impersonator of all time," and at worst a "large, soft, flabby and billowing superblonde who talks through her nostrils and whose laborious ambulations suggest that she has sore feet . . . [A] menace to art, if not to morals." The woman who portrayed sex the way she wanted to, for her own pleasure and according to her own view of the world, began to be elbowed out by men intent on reclaiming their prerogative to cast women as sexy as they thought fit.

Madonna

Between the two world wars, Western society briefly toyed with the idea of strong, independent women, and Mae West flourished until she came to be viewed as too vigorous a representation of feminine sexual independence. To save men from increasing self-doubt and confusion, the Hollywood censors shut Mae West down. West's successors, the tall, cool femmes fatales, retreated into Sphinx-like inscrutability, and men were free once more to create temptresses to reflect their fears and desires: chilling then childlike; freshly innocent or worldly wise. Whether they were women who ultimately knew their place or women who were eager to carve out more territory from the male domain, men were in control.

As women made strides towards independence during the latter half of the twentieth century, another bold, brassy female stepped to center stage. In the eighties, Madonna Louise Ciccone, a product of a strictly Catholic, tightly controlled, immigrant American upbringing, obliged. Whereas Mae West adopted a sexual persona and stubbornly stuck with it even as she aged, Madonna paraded a constantly changing lineup of provocative sexual roles across the stage. Mae West was Mae West was Mae West, but by Madonna's day, a woman could choose a persona to suit her purposes and her mood.

In her dress-up trunk of personas, the traditional male fantasies (schoolgirl, dominatrix) might excite her, or they might not. That was her choice, her territory, her delight. Surrounded by an unprecedented smorgasbord of sexual choices in the artistic underground of New York in the 1970s, she created an image all her own in the early 1980s, conscious that at any moment she could become a completely different character by drawing another costume from the theatrical possibilities laid before her.

Early in her career, Madonna was especially intrigued by the blending of traditional territories. She blurred gender distinctions, race distinctions, and connected religion and sex with a distinctly medieval verve. She was the Material Girl, the Boy Toy, the gangster's moll, the masturbating virgin bride. She wore her hair wild or severely pulled back. Underwear became outerwear. She dressed like a tart, a diva, a man. "I do not endorse a way of life," she said, "but describe one." At all times, Madonna was in control of the images she presented, orchestrating tours and dictating the choreography of her dances. Like Mae West, she relegated male performers to window dressing, dancing scenery that showcased her own electric presence.

For Madonna, the world was one huge sexual supermarket. She could browse the aisles of historical seduction, pull out items that caught her fancy, and whip up an original recipe of her own. Her main messages were power, control, and muscle. Hers was a vigorous, in-your-face sexuality that reminded women of their sexual power and encouraged them to embrace it in whatever ways best suited them. She was opening the door to an overt and flexible female sexuality that could accompany the advances women had made in other areas of their lives.

When Jean Harlow was dubbed the Platinum Blonde and Marilyn Monroe perfected her wiggling walk and wide-eyed gaze, the temptress image was a rigid man-made mold. Riding in the wake of feminist gains in

166

Britney Spears

· · · · · · · · · · · · · ·

AT THE END of the twentieth century, Britney Spears was the model for many young girls just turning the corner into womanhood. Her skimpy clothing showed off the preferred young female physique at the turn of the millennium: pert breasts, tight buns, and a washboard stomach accessorized with a navel ring. Her breasts were neither cantilevered nor in bondage, and the contouring of her stomach was achieved with diet and exercise rather than with whalebone or elastic. Even in an age acclimatized to the sight of naked female flesh, her low-rise waistband gave pause, the tantalizing glimpse of thong suggesting gift-packaging of the most intriguing part of her anatomy. There was nothing of the maternal in this party girl. No pillowy breasts in which to sink. No well-upholstered curves signaling fertility. Just pure, unadulterated girl-power. Yet even though Spears's stage persona exuded the brash self-confidence of a thoroughly modern young woman, those who control her image did not forget the legacy of the generations of temptresses before her. Dancing draped in a python and straddling a tiger at the MTV Video Music Awards in 2001, her stage persona drew on the age-old iconography of Eve and predatory womanhood to suggest the hidden powers of her sexual allure and her willingness to embrace it. As presented, she was toned, buff, and ready. The question is, whose desires was she there to satisfy? Those of liberated young women ready to take charge of their lives or those of eager young males on the lookout for their next thrill? Or both?

the twentieth century, Madonna underscored what women of her generation were beginning to learn: that their sexual natures need not be fixed. They did not have to accept a one-size-fits-all image. They could pick and choose. Women no longer had to be either Eve or Madonna; they could be both, one after the other or simultaneously. Now women could be the ones accentuating the attributes and deepening the shadows according to their own personal agendas. Armed with their new freedom, women began to claim for themselves their own personal fantasies of the temptress in their everyday lives.

Navel Art and the Home Striptease

At the beginning of the twenty-first century, the equilibrium between the sexes is relatively stable. This is not to say that the balance of power is equal or that men will not panic in the future, but that right here, right now, there is some space to experiment and room to breathe. Women, especially older women, are taking advantage of the relative calm. The issue of female sexual satisfaction is being openly discussed on daytime television talk shows. Jamie Lee Curtis posed for the September 2002 issue of *More* magazine stripped down to her sports bra and spandex shorts to show what her middle-aged body looks like before the lighting crews, makeup technicians, and airbrush experts get to work. A January 2000 *Ladies' Home Journal* article entitled "101 Ways to Sex Up Your Marriage" discussed ways in which wives might bring "more sizzle" into the bedroom—from the wives' point of view.

The good news for men is that frank discussions of women's sexual desire has combined with the images of sexual empowerment forged by performers such as Mae West and Madonna to create a new incarnation of the temptress. Instead of being a fantasy image projected onto women at the margins of society or an archetype who inhabits myths that men hear about but never experience, this new vision of the sexy seductress is constructed in the minds of men's long-term partners and is being given substance in private (or not-so-private) spaces before his very eyes.

The sinuous undulations of the belly dancer, with her whiff of harem and spice, are filling community halls across North America as the mothers of teenagers decide it's time to explore what their bodies—so long devoted to others—can do to make them feel more feminine. In early-twenty-first-century Hollywood, actor Sheila Kelley's workshops on pole dancing and lap dancing for beginners are filling up fast. Her studio is located on the property of her Hollywood home, and as her husband changes diapers in the house, he can hear the screams and whistles as women in their thirties and forties perfect their home-seduction routines. Kelley's interest in stripping began when she was researching her part in the 2000 movie *Dancing at the Blue Iguana*, and she got the idea for the workshops after putting on a private performance for her husband. She could not believe how much satisfaction she derived from a striptease originally intended for his delight.

Toni Bentley is a classically trained dancer and the author of *Sisters of Salome*, a book about early-twentieth-century interpreters of Salome's Dance of the Seven Veils, who became intrigued by the potentially explosive balance between power and exposure when women take off their clothes. As part of the research for her book, she found a nightclub in New York where she could experiment with what it felt like to strip before paying strangers. She decided on a stage costume of tight, sophisticated black velvet with very high heels.

To the gravelly tones of Leonard Cohen singing "Waiting for the Miracle," Bentley peeled her gown from her naked body, bending over, legs straight, to touch the floor. When all she was wearing was her red nail polish and high-heeled shoes, she paused for a moment, then stepped out of the dark pool of fabric at her feet. She stood tall, arching her back and raising her hands above her head. There was absolutely nothing between her and her audience but the energy created by their undivided attention. In that moment, she felt victorious, for she knew that for as long as she held their gaze, every man in the room was hers and hers alone. Through a performance that she described as being full of "grace and lewd intention," she felt she had gained the freedom to fly.

The sense of power that lingers long after a sexually charged performance may lurk in the most unlikely of places, just waiting to be uncovered. In the *9 Chickweed Lane* comic strip published on 12 September 2002, the demurely dressed main female character reveals to her teenage daughter, Edda: "Just for a hoot, I'm wearing a diamondback rattlesnake body suit under this." As Edda walks past the couch on which her mother's boyfriend is sitting, she casually remarks: "You're out of your depth, Mr. Boxer Shorts."

It's not foolproof, but accepting that sexual personas can be assumed and shed as a woman wants rather than as a man decides has allowed women to experiment without fear of being branded as loose. As women of a certain age remove the boundaries erected over generations between "girls who do" and "girls who don't," the temptress is making inroads in the bedrooms of the nation.

Meanwhile, in high school corridors, legions of young girls reveal naked flesh between the bottoms of their skimpy T-shirts and the ever-descending tops of their tight-fitting jeans. Their navels flash with rings, studs, and delicate chains with teardrop hearts. What are men to make of the next generation? One middle-aged newspaper columnist, acclimatized over the years to generous doses of cleavage, belly, and thighs in the media, admits to watching in dismay as the waistbands of barely pubescent girls descend perilously close to a point of no return as far as his hormones are concerned.

Have these young women no shame? Are they brainwashed by modern culture into thinking that they have no choice but to display themselves as overtly sexual beings? Or do they delight in confounding the men around them by displaying so much flesh that is not necessarily theirs for the taking? Are these young girls helplessly objectified by popular culture, or are they claiming control of their bodies and proudly displaying what is theirs as they see fit? Are they the next wave of liberated home strippers, or the next wave of women to be brainwashed by male-manipulated images of how men want their women to look?

THE FUTURE of the temptress depends on the balance of power between the sexes. If women aggressively push for more rights, overly defensive men will reject a female contribution to the temptress fantasy and sinister temptresses will once more stalk men's dreams. If men successfully reassert themselves, they will banish female reflections of desire and mold a comforting fantasy of their own. If, however, men accept women's progress toward equality, women who choose to explore their sexuality will continue to offer up their own visions of what a temptress can be. In this case, the temptress will become both accessible and tantalizing, a fantasy that accommodates both male and female desires, an infinitely arresting figure finally within reach.

Notes

Numbers at left refer to page numbers.

15   *The Alphabet of Ben Sira:* Translated in Stern and Mirsky, *Rabbinic Fantasies.*

15   *The Alphabet of Ben Sira:* Ibid.

18   "The Lai of Aristotle" by Henri d'Andeli: Translated by Stephen G. Nichols. In Flores, *Medieval Age*, pp. 320–30.

20   "You are [each] . . . not valiant enough to attack": Tertullian, "On the Apparel of Women," in Roberts and Donaldson, *The Ante-Nicene Fathers*, p. 14.

20   "The Prince of Darkness": *Acta Archelai*, chap. 10. Quoted in Evans, *Paradise Lost*, pp. 66–72.

21   Advice on avoiding women's seductive touch: Described in Abbot, *Celibacy*, p. 45.

28   It all started: For one version of Pandora's tale, see ll42–105 of "Works and Days," in Hesiod, *Homeric Hymns.*

30   One of Freud's followers: Ferenczi, *Thalassa.*

30   Odysseus manages this feat: For one version of this tale, see Books X and XII in Homer, *The Odyssey.*

35   Medusa's beauty: Much of Medusa's tale is recounted in Ovid, *Metamorphoses*, Book 4.

46   "prostitute queen": Propertius, *Poems*, p. 11.

46   Lucan: *Pharsalia*, Book 9.

46   Pliny: *Natural History*, Book 9, chap. 57, pp. 120–21.

48   Octavian was advancing his own cause: "The Story According to Octavius," in Hughes-Hallet, *Cleopatra*, pp. 36–69.

49   "It was as if he were": Plutarch, *Makers of Rome*, chap. 27.

51   "And it was now that": Plutarch, *Makers of Rome*, chap. 66.

52   Not one but many meals: "Antony," in Plutarch, *Lives.*

52   The logical extension: In his essay "Cleopatra Regina" published in *De Viris Illustribus*, Sextus Aurelius Victor wrote that Cleopatra was so beautiful "many men paid with their lives for a night with her." The story was revived by Alexander Pushkin in 1825. Quoted in Hughes-Hallet, *Cleopatra*, p. 233.

58   Wu Zhao: In Leon, *Uppity Women.*

62   "The prospect of possessing": Quoted in Hardwick, *Emma*, p. 23.

63   "[The spectator] sees": Goethe, *Italian Journey.*

65   "the favorite of the harem": Quoted in Lofts, *Emma*, p. 83.

66   "You seemed that wave": "Merlin and Vivien," in Tennyson, *Idylls of the King.*

66   "The pale blood of the wizard": Ibid.

68   "a little tigress": Mr. Grant. Quoted in *Sunderland Herald*, 13 August 1849, 5c1–2.

70 "a physical invitation": *Münchener Conversationsblatt*, 5 October 1843, 319C1–2.

71 "The sixty year old has awakened": Ludwig to Heinrich Baron von der Tann, 17 November 1846. Quoted in Corti, *Ludwig I von Bayern*, p. 465.

72 "she was lovely despite her rage": "Aus den Tagen von Lola Montez," Neue Deutsche Rundschau 1901, p. 927.

72 "genius of charm": Lewald, *Zwölf Bilder*, p. 351.

72 "perfection incarnate": Ludwig Simon, "L'extraordinaire aventure de Lola Montez." *Archives internationales de la danse*, Bibliothèque Nationale de France, Paris, October 1935, p. 135.

72 "You were born to be my misfortune": Ludwig, *Gedichte*.

73 "Up to now": *Cincinnati Gazette*, 2 March 1853, 2c3.

73 "liquid sweetness": *Montreal Daily Argus*, 29 August 1856, 2c1–2.

75 "If it were possible": H. Ashton Wolfe. Quoted in Newman, *Mata Hari*, p. 10.

81 "because women do feel themselves aggrieved": "The Seneca Falls Declaration of Sentiments." Reprinted in Stanton et al., *History*, p. 70.

84 "an eternal desire for": *Courier Français*. Quoted in Keay, *The Spy Who Never Was*, pp. 47–48.

84 "Vague rumours had reached me": "The Parisians of Paris," *The King*, 4 February 1905.

86 "would have gone through fire": Quoted in Wheelwright, *Fatal Lover*, p. 51.

88 Sir Basil . . . later wrote: Thomson, *Queer People*.

88 "I did what a woman does": Interrogation by Bouchardon, 28 February 1917. In *Dossier Mata Hari*, Service Historique de l'Armée de Terre, Château de Vincennes, Paris.

90 "The Zelle lady": Quoted in Wheelwright, *Fatal Lover*, p. 90.

90 "a sinister Salome": Maurice de Waleffe, "Après le chatiment de l'espionne," *Le Journal*, 27 July 1917.

90 lust for excitement: Steinhauer, *Steinhauer*.

90 "far more cunning": *La Belgique*, October 1915. Quoted in Thuliez, *Condemned to Death*, p. 163.

90 "How I would fasten my mouth": Freya in Ibanez, *Mare Nostrum*.

91 "to whip a cat": André Mornet. Quoted in "La Mata-Harisme," *Crapouillot*, 15 November 1952, pp. 39–42.

91 "crumpled heap of petticoats": Emile Massard. Quoted in "La véridique histoire de Mata Hari— l'Expiation," *La Liberté*, 13 December 1921.

94 "Metamorphoses of the Vampire": Baudelaire, *Poems*.

94 "A Fool there was": "The Vampire," in Kipling, *Complete Verse*.

106 "The doorbell rang": Barbara Brown. Quoted in Stenn, *Bombshell*, p. 17.

106 "Even at that age": Jada Leland. Quoted in Stenn, *Bombshell*, p. 22.

107 "Miss Harlean Carpenter": Selznick, *Private View*.

107 "They [the other pupils]": Scott, *Hollywood When Silents Were Golden*.

107 "We weren't told": Quoted in Skretvedt, *Laurel and Hardy*.

108 "Nudity was rarely seen": Loos, *Kiss Hollywood Good-bye*.

108 "Something for the boys": Bill Edmondson. Quoted in Stenn, *Bombshell*, p. 98.

109 "She made her entrance": William Bakewell. Quoted in Stenn, *Bombshell*, p. 55.

109 "How do you hold those things up?": Quoted in Kobal, *People Will Talk*.

109 "Why, dear, that dress . . . more coffee": Harlow, *Today Is Tonight*.

111 "some part of her": Zukor, *The Public Is Never Wrong*.

111 "a dancing flame": Arzner in *Hollywood: The Pioneers*, produced for Thames Television, London, by Kevin Brownlow and David Gill, n.d.

111 mantrap: *Variety*, 14 July 1926.

111 "loving" room . . . "Aw, gee": Tui Lorraine Bow, "The Mourning After: Memoirs of a Star-Crossed Spirit," unpublished manuscript. Quoted in Stenn, *Clara Bow*, p. 100.

111 "Lemme tell ya this": "Savage Just Episode in My Young Life, Declares Clara Bow," *Los Angeles Examiner*, 6 June 1926.

111 "[Harlow] was wearing": Artie Jacobson. Quoted in Stenn, *Clara Bow*, p. 179.

112 "she could flirt": *New York Times*, 12 July 1926.

112 "I've never taken dope": John Engstead. Quoted in Kobal, *People Will Talk*.

112 "[Monroe] got sex": Quoted in Zolotow, *Marilyn Monroe*.

112 "She toted a breast": *Night and Day*, 26 August 1937.

115 "an inner grace": Quoted in Ringgold, *Hayworth*, p. 12.

116 "Lamia": Keats, *Lamia*.

117 "tempestuous loveliness of terror": "On the Medusa of Leonardo da Vinci in the Florentine Gallery," line 33. Shelley, *Posthumous Poems*, pp. 139–40.

128 Her 42DD assets: Yalom, *Breast*, p. 192.

128 "I guess Ben doesn't like pink": Quoted in Buskin, *Blonde Heat*, p. 16.

132 "like a thunderstorm": Gary Johnson, "The Rise and Fall of the Feature-Length Western," *Images* [online journal]. <http://www.imagesjournal.com/issue06/infocus/western4.htm>.

158 "emanating from her body": Critic of Ohio run of *Sex*. Quoted in Leider, *Becoming Mae West*, p. 217.

158 "I like 'em tight": Quoted in Head, *The Dress Doctor*, p. 53.

158 "saw something in her middle": Sergeant Patrick Keneally. Quoted in West, *Goodness*, p. 95.

159 "Miss West's personality": Quoted in West, *Goodness*, pp. 97–98.

159 "what a hot fire is": "Flaming Mae," *New York Evening Telegram*, 18 April 1928.

159 "What do you do?" . . . "four different levels": Quinn, *Original Sin*.

159 "couldn't sing a lullaby": Bige, *Variety*, 14 February 1933.

159 "offering you tea and toast": Glenys Roberts. Quoted in Leonard, *Mae West*, p. 339.

159 "There was a terrific explosion": Leonard Hall, *Photoplay*. Quoted in Leonard, *Mae West*, p. 112.

160 "upholstered egg cup": Quoted in Leonard, *Mae West*, p. 68.

160 "very tasteful": Quoted in Leonard, *Mae West*, p. 63.

160 "I'm the girl who": Quoted in Leonard, *Mae West*, p. 135.

160 "When I am attracted to a man": Mae West, "SEX, More Sex, and the Cooler." Reprinted as "The Bad Girl of Broadway" in Alexander, *Outrageous Women*, pp. 323–46.

160 "In the films": Quoted in Chandler, *Ultimate Seduction*, p. 68.

161 "Sorry, baby": John Bright, "One of a Kind," *L.A. Weekly*, 16–22 July 1982, p. 18.

161 "She looks more like": Quoted in Leonard, *Mae West*, p. 147.

161 "a tribute to my sex appeal": Quoted in Leonard, *Mae West*, p. 230.

162 "Catherine was a great empress": Quoted in Leonard, *Mae West*, p. 247.

162 "My favorite audience": Quoted in Leonard, *Mae West*, p. 329.

162 "the only girl": *I'm No Angel*. Hays Office files, Margaret Herrick Library, Academy of Motion Picture Arts and Sciences, Beverly Hills.

163 "as a last resort": Ibid.

163 "I never worked with anyone": *Picturegoer*, 30 December 1933.

164 "America's wet dream": John Bright, "One of a Kind," *L.A. Weekly*, 16–22 July 1982, p. 18.

164 "the greatest female impersonator": "The Decline of the West," *Vanity Fair*, May 1934.

164 "large, soft, flabby": Percy Hammond, "Is There No Flit?" *New York Herald Tribune*, 4 October 1931.

166 "I do not endorse": Quoted in Jock McGregor, "Madonna: Icon of Postmodernity," 1997. Via the Facing the Challenge Web site <http://www.facingthechallenge.org/madonna.htm>.

171 "grace and lewd intention": Bentley, *Sisters*, p. 12.

172 One middle-aged: Russell Smith, "Cleavage, fine. Bellies, well okay. But groins?" Toronto *Globe and Mail*, 21 September 2002, R6.

Bibliography

Abbott, Elizabeth. *A History of Celibacy*. Toronto: HarperCollins, 1999.

Ackerman, Diane. *A Natural History of Love*. New York: Random House, 1994.

Aesop. *Aesop's Fables*. London: Heinemann, 1912.

Alexander, Gemma, ed. *The Mammoth Book of Heroic and Outrageous Women*. London: Robinson, 1999.

Aristophanes. *Volume III, Birds, Lysistrata, Women at the Thesmophoria*, trans. Jeffrey Henderson. Loeb Classical Library Series No. 179. Cambridge, Mass.: Harvard University Press, 2000.

Aurelius Victor, Sextus. *De Viris Illustribus*. London: n.p., 1759.

Bade, Patrick. *Femme Fatale: Images of Evil and Fascinating Women*. New York: Mayflower Books, 1979.

Baudelaire, Charles. *Baudelaire: Poems*. Everyman's Library Pocket Poets. New York: Knopf, 1993.

Bentley, Toni. *Sisters of Salome*. New Haven, Conn.: Yale University Press, 2002.

Browne, Porter Emerson. *A Fool There Was*. New York: The H.K. Fly Company, 1909.

Buskin, Richard. *Blonde Heat: The Sizzling Screen Career of Marilyn Monroe*. New York: Watson-Guptill, 2001.

Cameron, Julia Margaret. *Illustrations to Tennyson's "The Idylls of the King" and Other Poems*. London: Henry S. King and Company, 1875.

Chandler, Charlotte. *The Ultimate Seduction*. Garden City, N.Y.: Doubleday, 1984.

Corti, Egon Cäsar Conte. *Ludwig I von Bayern*. Munich: Bruckmann, 1937.

Dijkstra, Bram. *Evil Sisters: The Threat of Female Sexuality and the Cult of Manhood*. New York: Knopf, 1996.

Dijkstra, Bram. *Idols of Perversity: Fantasies of Feminine Evil in Fin-de-Siecle Culture*. Oxford: Oxford University Press, 1986.

Eisler, Riane. *The Chalice and the Blade: Our History, Our Future*. New York: HarperCollins, 1987.

Eisler, Riane. *Sacred Pleasure: Sex, Myth, and the Politics of the Body*. New York: HarperCollins, 1995.

Evans, J.M. *Paradise Lost and the Genesis Tradition*. Oxford: Oxford University Press, 1913.

Ferenczi, Sandor. *Thalassa: Theory of Genitality*. New York: W.W. Norton, 1968.

Flores, Angel, ed. *The Medieval Age*. Laurel Masterpieces of World Literature. New York: Dell, 1963.

Goethe, Johann Wolfgang von. *Italian Journey, 1786–1788*, trans. W.H. Auden and Elizabeth Mayer. New York: Penguin, 1992.

Golden, Eve. *Vamp: The Rise and Fall of Theda Bara*. Vestal, N.Y.: Emprise, 1996.

Grant, Michael. *Cleopatra*. London: Weidenfeld & Nicholson, 1972.

Hardwick, Mollie. *Emma, Lady Hamilton: A Study*. London: Cassell, 1969.

Harlow, Jean. *Today Is Tonight*. New York: Dell, 1965.

Harvey, James. *Movie Love in the Fifties*. New York: Knopf, 2001.

Head, Edith. *The Dress Doctor*. Boston: Little, Brown, 1959.

Hesiod. *The Homeric Hymns and Homerica*, trans. Hugh G. Evelyn-White. Loeb Classical Library Series No. 57. Cambridge, Mass.: Harvard University Press, 1936.

Hickman, Tom. *The Sexual Century*. London: Carlton, 1999.

Homer. *The Odyssey*, trans. Samuel Butler. New York: Barnes and Noble Books, 1994.

Hughes-Hallett, Lucy. *Cleopatra: Histories, Dreams and Distortions*. London: Bloomsbury, 1990.

Ibanez, Vicente Blasco. *Mare Nostrum*. London: Constable, 1920.

Jordan, Ted. *Norma Jean: My Secret Life with Marilyn Monroe*. New York: William Morrow, 1989.

Keats, John. *Lamia, Isabella, the Eve of St. Agnes, and Other Poems*. Banbury, U.K.: Woodstock Books, 2001.

Keay, Julia. *The Spy Who Never Was: The Life and Loves of Mata Hari*. London: Michael Joseph, 1987.

Kipling, Richard. *The Complete Verse*. London: Kyle Cathie, 1990.

Kobal, John. *People Will Talk*. New York: Knopf, 1985.

Leaming, Barbara. *If This Was Happiness: A Biography of Rita Hayworth*. New York: Viking, 1989.

Leider, Emily Wortis. *Becoming Mae West*. New York: Farrar Straus & Giroux, 1997.

Leon, Vicki. *Uppity Women of Medieval Times*. Berkeley, Calif.: Conari, 1997.

Leonard, Maurice. *Mae West: Empress of Sex*. Secaucus, N.J.: Carol, 1992.

Lewald, Fanny. *Zwölf Bilder nach dem Leben*. Berlin: Janke, 1888.

Lofts, Norah. *Emma Hamilton*. London: Michael Joseph, 1978.

Loos, Anita. *Kiss Hollywood Good-bye*. New York: Viking, 1974.

Lucan. *Pharsalia*, trans. Jane Wilson Joyce. Masters of Latin Literature Series. Ithaca, N.Y.: Cornell University Press, 1993.

Ludwig I. *Gedichte*. Bayerisches Hauptstaatsarchiv, Munich, Abteilung III, Geheimes Hausarchiv.

McElvaine, Robert S. *Eve's Seed: Biology, the Sexes, and the Course of History*. New York: McGraw-Hill, 2001.

Montreynaud, Florence. *Love: A Century of Love and Passion*. Evergreen Series. Koln: Benedikt Taschen Verlag, 1998.

Mordden, Ethan. *Movie Star: A Look at the Women Who Made Hollywood*. New York: St. Martin's, 1983.

Morris, Desmond. *The Human Sexes: A Natural History of Man and Woman*. New York: St. Martin's, 1997.

Nabokov, Vladimir. *Lolita*. New York: Putnam, 1958.

Newman, Bernard. *Inquest on Mata Hari*. London: Robert Hale, 1956.

Norris, Pamela. *Eve: A Biography*. London: Macmillan, 1998.

Olmer, Georges. *Salon de 1886*. Paris: L. Baschet, 1886.

Ovid. *The Metamorphoses*, trans. Allen Mandelbaum. San Diego, Calif.: Harcourt, 1993.

Pagels, Elaine. *Adam, Eve, and the Serpent*. New York: Random House, 1988.

Petersen, James R., et al. *The Century of Sex: Playboy's History of the Sexual Revolution, 1900–1999*. New York: Grove, 1999.

Phillips, John A. *Eve: The History of an Idea*. San Francisco: Harper & Row, 1984.

Pliny. *Natural History, Vol. III, Books 8–11*, trans. H. Rackham. Loeb Classical Library Series No. 353. Cambridge, Mass.: Harvard University Press, 1940.

Plutarch. *Makers of Rome*, trans. Ian Scott-Kilvert. Harmondsworth, U.K.: Penguin, 1965.

Plutarch. *Plutarch's Lives*, trans. John Dryden. New York: The Modern Library, 2001.

Propertius. *The Poems, Book III*, trans. W.G. Shepherd. Harmondsworth, U.K.: Penguin, 1985.

Quinn, Anthony. *The Original Sin: A Self-Portrait*. London: W.H. Allen, 1972.

Ringgold, Gene. *The Films of Rita Hayworth: The Legend and Career of a Love Goddess*. Secaucus, N.J.: The Citadel Press, 1974.

Roberts, Alexander, and James Donaldson, eds. *The Ante-Nicene Fathers: Translations of the Writings of the Fathers Down to A.D. 32*, vol. 4. Buffalo: The Christian Literature Publishing Company, 1857.

Rosen, Marjorie. *Popcorn Venus: Women, Movies, and the American Dream*. London: Peter Owen, 1973.

Scott, Evelyn F. *Hollywood When Silents Were Golden*. New York: McGraw-Hill, 1972.

Selznick, Irene Mayer. *A Private View*. New York: Knopf, 1983.

Seymour, Bruce. *Lola Montez: A Life*. New Haven, Conn.: Yale University Press, 1996.

Shelley, Percy Bysshe. *Posthumous Poems of Percy Bysshe Shelley*, ed. Mary W. Shelley. London: John and Henry L. Hunt, 1824.

Skretvedt, Randy. *Laurel and Hardy: The Magic Behind the Movies*. Potomac, Md.: Moonstone Press, 1987.

Stanton, E.C., S.B. Anthony, and M.J. Gage, eds. *History of Women's Suffrage*, vol. 1. New York: National Woman Suffrage Association, 1881.

Steinhauer, Gustave. *Steinhauer: The Kaiser's Master Spy As Told By Himself*, ed. S.T. Felstead. London: John Lane, 1930.

Stenn, David. *Bombshell: The Life and Death of Jean Harlow*. New York: Doubleday, 1993.

Stenn, David. *Clara Bow: Running Wild*. New York: Doubleday, 1988.

Stern, David, and Mark Jay Mirsky, eds. *Rabbinic Fantasies: Imaginative Narratives from Classical Hebrew Literature*. Yale Judaica Series. New Haven, Conn.: Yale University Press, 1998.

Stoker, Bram. *Dracula*. New York: New American Library, 1965.

Taylor, G. Rattray. *Sex in History*. London: Thames & Hudson, 1953.

Tennyson, Alfred, Lord. *Idylls of the King*, ed. J. M. Gray. New Haven, Conn.: Yale University Press, 1983.

Thomson, Basil. *Queer People*. London: Hodder and Stoughton, 1922.

Thuliez, Louise. *Condemned to Death*. London: Methuen, 1934.

Walker, Alexander. *Sex in the Movies: The Celluloid Sacrifice*. Harmondsworth, U.K.: Penguin, 1968.

West, Mae. *Goodness Had Nothing to Do With It*. New York: Manor Books, 1976.

Wheelwright, Julie. *The Fatal Lover: Mata Hari and the Myth of Women in Espionage*. London: Collins & Brown, 1992.

Wilde, Oscar. *Salome*. Boston: John W. Luce, 1907.

Wolf, Naomi. *The Beauty Myth*. New York: William Morrow, 1991.

Wollstonecraft, Mary. *A Vindication of the Rights of Woman*. New York: W.W. Norton, 1988.

Yalom, Marilyn. *A History of the Breast*. New York: Ballantine, 1997.

Yalom, Marilyn. *A History of the Wife*. New York: HarperCollins, 2001.

Zolotow, Maurice. *Marilyn Monroe*. New York: Harcourt Brace, 1960.

Zukor, Adolph, with Dale Kramer. *The Public Is Never Wrong*. New York: Putnam, 1953.

Illustration Credits

Index

Numbers in **boldface** indicate illustrations

Adam, 16, 17, 19–20, **20–21,** 29
Agnew, Lady, 100, **101**
Alexander the Great, 18, 43, 47
Alphabet of Ben Sira, The, 15, 16
And God Created Woman (movie 1956), 130, **130**
Anthony, Saint, 25
Aristophanes, 39
Aristotle, 18, **18**
Arzner, Dorothy, 111
Athena, 35, 37
Athens, 39
Atlas, 37

Bancroft, Anne, 135–40, **138**
Bara, Theda, **50,** 51, 96–99, **96, 97**
Bardot, Brigitte, 130, **130**
Basic Instinct (movie 1992), **146,** 147–54, **153**
Baudelaire, Charles, 94
Beardsley, Aubrey, 78, **79**
Ben (character). *See* Braddock, Benjamin
Bentley, Toni, 170–71
Bernhardt, Sarah, 100
Blue Angel, The (movie 1930), **98,** 99, 102–3
Body Heat (movie 1981), **vi,** 1–4
Bond, James (character), **144,** 145

Bone, Henry, 58, **59**
Bonney, Anne, 4
Boucher, François, **56,** 57
Boulanger, Gustave, 4, **5**
Bow, Clara, **110,** 111, 112, **113**
Braddock, Benjamin (character), 136–40, **138**
Bright, John, 161
Brooks, Romaine, 100
Brosnan, Pierce, **144,** 145
Browne, Porter Emerson, 95–96
Burne-Jones, Philip, 94

Cagney, James, 109
Cameron, Julia Margaret, **66**
Carpenter, Harlean. *See* Harlow, Jean
Catherine Was Great (play 1944), 162
Cellini, Benvenuto, **38,** 39
Charybdis, 30
Chrysaor, 37
Ciccone, Madonna Louise. *See* Madonna
Circe, 30–32, **33**
Cleopatra, 13, **40,** 41–55, **43, 47, 50, 55,** 57, 59, 86, 90
Cleopatra (movie 1917), **50,** 51; (movie 1934), 54, **55**
Close, Glenn, 155
Colbert, Claudette, 54, **55**
Collier, John, **14,** 15
Cooper, Gary, 111
Cranach, Lucas, the Elder, **6,** 7

Curran, Nick (character), 148–54, **153**
Curtis, Jamie Lee, 169

d'Andeli, Henri, 18
Davis, Marion, 112
De Mille, Cecile B., 54
Delilah, 82, **82,** 90
Diamond Lil (play 1928), 159
Dietrich, Marlene, **98,** 99, 102–3, **103,** 116
Dietrichson, Mrs. (character), 117–22, **119**
Double Indemnity (movie 1944), 117–22, **119**
Double Whoopee (movie 1929), 107
Douglas, Michael, 148–54, **153,** 155
Dracula, 94
Dury, Georg, 68, **69**

Eastwood, Clint, 155
Echidna, 121
Eden, Garden of, 16, 19, **20,** 22–24, **23**
Epimetheus, 27, 28–29
Eve, 19–20, **20–21,** 22–24, **23,** 168

Fanny (wife of Nelson), 64
Farrell, Johnny (character), 122–24
Fatal Attraction (movie 1987), 155
Ferdinand, King (of Naples), 62

Fetherstonaugh, Sir Harry, 60–61
film noir, 10, 115–25, 148, 152, 163
Fiorentino, Linda, 155
Fleming, Victor, 108
Fool There Was, A (movie 1915),
    96, 96–97
Fool There Was, A (play 1909),
    95–96
Ford, Glenn, 122–24
Fuller, Loïe, 76
Fulvia (wife of Mark Anthony),
    46, 47

Gable, Clark, 112
Gennari, Bartolomeo, **40,** 41
Gentlemen Prefer Blondes (movie
    1953), 132
Gilbert, Eliza. *See* Montez, Lola
Gilda (movie 1946), 122–25, **124**
Gillray, James, 64, **65**
Glyn, Elinor, 111
Goethe, Johann Wolfgang von,
    63
Goodman, Theodosia. *See* Bara,
    Theda
Graduate, The (movie 1967),
    136–40, **138**
Grant, Cary, 163
Greene, Graham, 112
Greville, the Honorable Charles
    Francis, 61–62
Gus (character). See Moran, Gus

Hacker, Arthur, 32, **92,** 93
Hall, Leonard, 159
Hamilton, Emma, 58–67, **59,**
    65, 75

Hamilton, Sir William, 62, 63,
    64, 65, **65,** 67
Harlow, Jean, **104,** 105, 106–9,
    108, 111, 112, 113
Hayworth, Rita, **114,** 115, 122–25,
    124
Hearst, William Randolph, 112
Heavy Metal, 22, 24
Hell's Angels (movie 1930),
    108–9
Hephaestus, 28
Hercules, 53, **53**
Hermes, 28, 32, 37, 53
Herod Antipas, 78, 80
Herodias, 78, 80
Hesiod, 29
Hilarion, Saint, **24,** 25
Hildebrandt, Greg, 22, **23**
Hoffman, Dustin, 136–40, **138**
Hughes, Howard, 108–9, 132
Humbert, Humbert (character),
    140–43
Hurt, William, 1–3

I'm No Angel (movie 1933), 162,
    164
Ingres, Jean Auguste Dominique,
    44–45, 45
Iron Man (movie 1931), 109

Jacobson, Artie, 111
Jannings, Emil, 102–3
Jerome, Saint, 25
John the Baptist, 78, 80
Johnston, David Claypoole,
    70, 71
Julius Caesar, 42–44, 47

Kalle, Major Arnold von, 88
Keats, John, 116–17
Kelley, Sheila, 170
Keyes, Barton (character), 118,
    120
Kipling, Rudyard, 94–95
Klee, Paul, 27
Kubrick, Stanley, 140

Ladoux, Captain Georges, 86,
    87, 88
Lady Lou (character), 163, 164
Lamia (poem 1819), 116–17
Last Seduction, The (movie
    1994), 155
Leighton, Frederic, **36**
Lilith, **14,** 15–17,
Liszt, Franz, 71, 72
Little Egypt (dancer), 78
Lola Lola (character), **98,** 99,
    102–3, 116
Lolita (movie 1962), 140, **141;**
    (movie 1997), **134**
Lolita (novel 1955), 135, 140–43
Long, Edwin Longsden, 42, **43**
Love Happy (movie 1949), 128
Lucan, 46
Ludwig I, King (of Bavaria),
    71–73
Lyon, Ben, 128
Lyon, Sue, 140, **141**
Lysistrata (play 411 BCE), 39

Mackennal, Edgar Bertram, 31
MacLeod, Rudolph, 83–84
MacMurray, Fred, 117–20, 150
Macready, George, 122–23

Madonna, 164, **165,** 165–69, **167**

Mamoulian, Rouben, 115, 125

Mansfield, Jayne, 128, **129**

Marceau, Sophie, **144**

Marcus Agrippa, 51

Maria Carolina, Queen (of
    Naples), 62–63, 64

Mark Antony, 44–51, 53, 54

Maslov, Vladimir de, 87

Mata Hari, **74,** 75, 83–91, **87**

Medusa, 35–38, **38,** 39

Merlin, 66, **66**

mermaids, 36, **36.** *See also* Sirens

Michelangelo Buonarroti, 19,
    20–21, 22

Monroe, Marilyn, **ii,** 113, **126,** 127

Montez, Lola, 67–73, **69, 70,
    72,** 75

Moran, Gus (character), 150, 151,
    152, 154

Mornet, Lieutenant André,
    89–90

Mundson, Ballin (character),
    122–23

Nabokov, Vladimir, 135, 140–43

Nathan, George Jean, 161

Neff, Walter (character), 117–20,
    150

Nelson, Lord Horatio, 63–65, 66

Nimue. *See* Vivien

9 Chickweed Lane, 171

Oboler, Arch, 163

Octavia (wife of Mark Antony),
    47, 49

Octavian, 44, 46, 47, 48–52, 53, 54

Odysseus, 30–34, **34–35,** 35, 37,
    119, 145

Oedipus, 121, **121**

Omphale, 53, **53**

Outlaw, The (movie 1943),
    132, **133**

Pandora, **26,** 27–29

Papety, Dominique Louis, **24,**
    25

Pegasus, 37

Pelopponesian War, 39

Percival, Sir, **92,** 93

Pericles, 39

Perseus, 35–38, **38,** 39

Phyllis, 18, **18**

Phyrne, 4, **5**

Play Misty for Me (movie 1971),
    155, **155**

Pliny, 46, 52

Plutarch, 49, 51, 52

Pompadour, Madame de, 58

Pompey the Great, 42

Poseidon, 35, 38

Prometheus, 28

Propertius, 46

Public Enemy (movie 1931), **104,**
    105, **108,** 109

Quilty, Clare (character), 143

Quinn, Anthony, 159, 160

Racine, Ned (character), 1–3

Rackham, Arthur, 30, **31**

Rath, Professor (character),
    102–3

Red Dust (movie 1932), 108

Red-Headed Woman (movie
    1932), 108

Reznicek, Ferdinand van, 8, **9**

Ricketts, Charles, **121**

Robinson, Edward G., 118, 120

Robinson, Elaine (character),
    137, 139, 140

Robinson, Mrs. (character),
    135–40, **138**

Romney, George, 61

Rops, Félicien, 31, 32, **33**

Rouffio, Paul-Albert, 82, **82**

Rousseau, Henri, 22

Rowena, **12,** 13

Rubinstein, Ida, 100

Russell, Jane, 132, **133**

Salome, 76–80, **77, 79**

Salome (play 1893), 76, 78

Samson, 82, **82**

Saratoga (movie 1937), 112

Sargent, John Singer, 100, **101**

Saturday Night Kid, The (movie
    1929), 111

Scudda Hoo! Scudda Hay!
    (movie 1947), 128

Scylla, 30

Sedan, Rolfe, 107–8

serpent, **14,** 15, 19, **20, 23,** 116–17

Seven-Year Itch, The (movie
    1955), 127–28, 131–32

Sex (play 1926), 158, 159

She Done Him Wrong (movie
    1933), 163, 164

Shamroy, Leon, 112

Sherman, Lowell, 161, 164

Simeon, Saint, 25

Sin (movie 1915), **97,** 99

Sirens, 30–34, **34–35,** 36, 37, 41, 139, 145, 157. *See also* mermaids

snake. *See* serpent

Sparta, 39

Spears, Britney, 168, **168**

Sphinx, the, 121, **121**

St. Cyr, Lili, 129

Stanwyck, Barbara, 117–22, **119**

Steinhauer, Gustave, 90

Stoker, Bram, 94

Stone, Sharon, **146,** 147, 148–54, **153**

Strauss, Richard, 78

Stuart, Miranda, 4

suffragettes, 81

Swain, Dominique, **134**

temptress, by era: overview, 4–13; in Greek mythology, 27–38, 81, 83, 121; in classical Greece, 39; in Hebrew thought, 22, 24, 39; in Bible, 19–21, 76–80, 81, 82; in Roman times, 41–54; in early Christian thought, 22, 24–25, 39; in Jewish folklore, 15–17; in medieval tales, 18, 66, 83, 93; in 1700s, 58–67; in 1800s, 67–73; in Victorian age, 75–85, 93–94; around WWI,

85–91, 95–99, 100; in 1920s, 105–6, 111; in 1930s, 99–103, 106–13; 157–64; around WWII, 115–25; in 1950s, 127–32; in 1960s, 135–45; in 1970s, 155; in 1980s, 155, 165–69; in 1990s, 145, 148–54, 155, 165–69; in 2000, 169–72; future of, 172

temptress, by type: bombshell, 105–13; courtesan, 7, 75, 85–86; dominatrix, 18, 31, 32, 33, 52, 53, 167; enchantress, 27–38; exotic, 41–52, 65, 83–85; femme fatale, 1–4, 10, 99, 102–3, 115–25, 149; "It" girl, 111, 112; mistress, 7, 57–73; nymphet, 76–78, 80, 135, 140–43, 172; nympho-maniac, 15–25, 54; older woman, 135–40; psychopath, 11, 52, 147–55; sex kitten, 8, 127–33; spy, 82, 87–91, 145; stripper, 78–80, 170–71; woman in charge of image, 11, 157–72; vamp, 10–11, 54, 94–97, 100–1, 108

Tennyson, Alfred, Lord, 66

Tertullian, 20

Thomson, Sir Basil, 88

Tira (character), 161, 162, 163, 164

Toudouze, Edouard, 76, **77**

Toulouse-Lautrec, Henri de, 76

Tramell, Catherine (character), **146,** 147, 148–54, **153**

Truth or Dare (movie 1991), 164, **165**

Turner, Kathleen, **vi,** 1–4

Typhon, 121

Ulysses. *See* Odysseus

Vallejo, Boris, **26,** 27

Vivien, 66, **66**

Walker, Maddy (character), 1–4

Walter, Jessica, **155**

Waterhouse, John William, **34–35,** 35

West, Mae, **156,** 157–64, **161,** 165

Wilde, Oscar, 76, 78

Wollstonecraft, Mary, 81

World Is Not Enough, The (movie 1999), **144**

Wu Zhao, 58

Zelle, Margaretha Geertruida. *See* Mata Hari

Zeus, 28, 35, 37

Zukor, Adolph, 111